School Resources and Performance in Developing Countries: A Resource-Based Perspective

Christopher B Mugimu
College of Education and External Studies, Makerere University
He is the chairman of the CCOED International, a consultancy firm based in Uganda and Rwanda.

COPYRIGHT © 2011 CHRISTOPHER B MUGIMU

MK PUBLISHERS LIMITED

ISBN: 9970-04-570-9

CONTENTS

PREFACE

CHAPTER ONE: PREAMBLE: SCHOOL RESOURCES, EDUCATIONAL QUALITY AND EFFECTIVENESS

Quality of Education	1
Educational Effectiveness Studies and School Resources	4
EE Studies in Industrialized Countries	5
EE Studies in Developing Countries	9
Limitations of EE Studies in Developing Countries	10
Physical Resources	11
Financial Resources	17
Human Resources	18
Resources and Secondary Education in Developing Countries	20
Conclusion	21

CHAPTER TWO: RESOURCE-BASED VIEW: LOCAL PERSPECTIVES

Emerging Theory	24
Resource Attributes: Superior Organization Performance	26
Value	27
Rareness	28
Inimitability	28
Non-Substitutability	30
Exploitable by the organization	30
RBV Empirical Studies	31
RBV Studies in Educational Organizations	31
Applying RBV at the Secondary School Level	32
Conclusion	32

CHAPTER THREE: STATUS OF SECONDARY EDUCATION IN UGANDA

The Impact of UPE Policy on Secondary Education in Uganda	33
Private Versus Government-Aided Secondary Schools	37
Rapid expansion of private sector and resources	39
Market-driven education and resources	39
Government-aided secondary schools and resources	40
Selective secondary school	40
Boarding versus secondary schools	41
Conclusion	42

CHAPTER FOUR: STATUS OF SCHOOL PERFORMANCE, PUBLIC EXAMINATION AND RESOURCES

Public Examinations as a Measure of Educational Quality	44
Public Examinations in Uganda	45
Public Examinations: A National Policy Makers' Perspective	46

Examination Format	47
General Implications of Public Examinations for Students	48
Implications of Public Examinations for Schools: a Practitioner's Perspective	49
Financing Examinations	49
Examination Strategies at School Level	49
Implications of Public Examinations	50
Use of Public Examination Results at National Level Educational Planning	50
Conclusion	51

CHAPTER FIVE: METHODOLOGY

Resource Model, Hypotheses and Variables	53
Hypotheses	53
Dependent Variable	55
Independent Variables	56
Research Design	59
Data Collection	60
Sample Design	60
Instrumentation	61
Collecting National Exam Data	62
Limitations of the Data	63
Data Analysis	64
Conclusion	65

CHAPTER SIX: FINDINGS AND RESULTS

Demographic and Contextual School Factors	66
Status of Secondary School Resources in Mukono Uganda	69
Status of Financial Resources	69
Descriptive Statistics and Status of Physical Resources	70
Descriptive Statistics of Human Resources	71
Status of Secondary School Performance Mukono Uganda	74
Correlational Relationships Between Variables on School Performance	79
Regression Modeling Results	81
Conclusion	88

CHAPTER SEVEN: THEORETICAL AND PRACTICAL IMPLICATIONS OF RBV, SUMMARYAND CONCLUSIONS

Summary of the Study	89
Regression Model 8 Results	90
Theoretical and Policy Implications	91
Theoretical Implication of Using RBV/VRISE	91
The Practical Implications of RBV	92
Apparent Inconsistencies with RBV	95
Resource Sharing	96
Overcoming Resource Barriers	96
Interpretation of Apparent RBV Inconsistencies	97

Beyond the Production Function Model	97
The RBV Solution	100
Practical Policy Implications and Future Research	100
General Conclusions	102
Lessons Learned Through this Study	103
Conclusion	104

REFERENCES 105

APPENDIX A: SUMMARY OF RBV EMPIRICAL STUDIES 124

APPENDIX B: FOUR-PART SURVEY

SSSS-2003: Personnel Survey (Part 1)	125
SSSS-2003: Headmaster Survey (Part 2)	132
SSSS-2003:Deputy Headmaster Survey (Part 3)	145
SSSS-2003: Additional Information (Part 4)	157

ACRONYMS

CDF	Capital Development Funds
EE	Capitation Grants
EE	Educational Effectiveness
IIEP	International Institute for Educational Planning
NGO	Non-Governmental Organization
RBV	Resource-Based View
SSSS	Secondary School Site Survey
UACE	Uganda Advanced Certificate of Education
UCE	Uganda Certificate of Education
MOES	Ministry of Education and Sports
UNEB	Uganda National Examination Board
UPE	Universal Primary Education
UPLE	Uganda Primary Leaving Examination
UShs	Uganda Shilling
UNESCO	United Nations Educational, Scientific and Cultural Organization
VRISE	Valuable, Rare, Inimitable, Non-Substitutable, and Exploitable by the Organization

PREFACE

SCHOOL RESOURCES AND PERFORMANCE IN DEVELOPING COUNTRIES: A RESOURCE-BASED PERSPECTIVE

While good facilities and resources are assumed to affect the quality of teaching and school performance, findings from the growing body of research about resources and school performance remain obscure and highly contested. A central question in effective schooling research is to what extent do resources translate into school performance particularly in under-resourced schools in developing countries. Grounded in the strategic Resource-Based View theory, this book presents recent research offering new insights on understanding school resources and performance in developing countries and at the same time being sensitive to diverse cultural contexts. The RBV theory suggests that specific resources and capabilities can lead to superior performance in business organizations. This book discusses how the RBV perspective can be applied in education sector to inform theory and practice on resources and school performance. Much of this book draws on datasets consisting of school-level resources and school performance as measured by aggregated UCE exam scores in sixty three secondary schools.

The findings of this study are mixed. While some results of this study indicated that the three kinds of resources (i.e. financial, physical, and human) contributed to performance in secondary schools in Uganda, particular kinds of resources contributed more to school performance than others and the size of their effect differed widely. This research also revealed the concept of resource sharing and satellite schools and the need for policy makers to extend their way of thinking in this direction. If educators and policy makers can identify critical resources that best contribute to student learning, then schools could be encouraged to invest in, nurture, and maintain these particular resources.

This strategic focus would allow schools, especially in developing countries to use their current meager resources more efficiently and effectively to maximize benefits to students hence improve their performance. Chapter one presents the introduction to resources in education. Chapter two covers the RBV theory and how it can be applied in the field of education especially about resources and school performance. Chapter three presents the demographic and contextual factors in the study. Chapter four discusses the status of secondary education and resources. Chapter five covers the methodology used in this case study. Chapter six discusses the status of secondary education and school performance. Chapter seven discusses the theoretical and practical implications of RBV in general and in particular focuses on resource sharing and satellite schools as well as conclusions.

ACKNOWLEDGEMENTS

The author wishes to express gratitude to all individuals that rendered help and support in numerous ways that culminated into the accomplishment of this project. I wish to thank my faculty committee members at Brigham Young University for their efforts to ensure that I completed this project in a timely manner. Special appreciation is dedicated to Dr. Steven J. Hite for the mentorship and guidance extended to me, right from the initial stages of this project and throughout the whole writing process. Dr. Julie M. Hite, her support and encouragement was fundamental for me to be able to complete this project.

Further, I wish to extend my appreciation to the primary editor of this manuscript, Dr. Josetta Ashford for reading through several drafts of this manuscript. Her comments have been extremely helpful. I wish to acknowledge Dr. Sterling Hilton for his time and technical advice put into this project. Dr. Vance Randall, I wish to register my heartfelt appreciation for the support throughout all the graduate school years.

I cannot forget my wife Susan and our children Margaret, Norah, Caroline, Deana, and Ammon for their constant companionship, encouragement, support, and empathy throughout this agonizing experience of writing. Finally, I wish to express gratitude and appreciation to my parents late Efulaimu B. Ssentamu and Mrs. Lovinsa Nagita Ssentamu, who provided the foundation of my education. As they taught me by example the right work ethics and the value of being patient without this legacy, in no way, I would have succeeded.

CHAPTER ONE

PREAMBLE: SCHOOL RESOURCES, EDUCATIONAL QUALITY AND EFFECTIVENESS

If schools are to be not just places where the young are placed for a period, but institutions where they are prepared for life, quality is at the heart of the matter (UNESCO, 2001, p. 66).

The central question confronting educators in every society is how to provide quality education when school resources are scarce. In recent years, stakeholders in education, in both industrialized and developing countries have increasingly demanded effective schooling and quality education for their disadvantaged youth (Hallak & Caillods, 1995; Watkins, Watt, & Buston, 2001). Providing adequate effective schooling opportunities for all the world's children is an overwhelming challenge to most governments, particularly those of developing countries (Atchoarena & Hite, 2001; Caillods & Postlethwaite, 1995; Lockheed & Levin, 1993). While most governments in developing countries have focused on improving access and quality for universal basic education, to a great extent, they have ignored secondary education. Even where universal basic education is realized, we should note that it is only a first vital step, not enough without excellent provisions for secondary education. The students cannot achieve their full potential and become competitive in the global job market without access to quality secondary education.

QUALITY OF EDUCATION

> Quality education is a public service and a social good that shapes the identities of individuals and raises the aspirations of societies. ...It equips all people, women and men, to be fully participating members of their own communities and also citizens of the world (UNESCO, 2003b, p. 1-2).

Increasing the quality of education has become more of a global effort to ensure that resources are made available to enable all the worlds' children gain access to educational experience of acceptable standards (Makwati, Audinos, & Lairez, 2003; Watkins, et al., 2001). Without access to quality education, children cannot learn the basic skills and knowledge they need to become responsible citizens in order to contribute to the increasingly growing global community.

Delegates to the Ministerial Round Table on Quality Education meeting, held in Paris, observed: "Quality education is a tool to overcome social disadvantages because in addition to being a human right, it is a means to fulfill other rights" (UNESCO, 2003b, p. 1). Quality education is also an essential avenue to improve equity, equality, and the quality of life (CIDA, 2002; Psacharopoulos, 2000; Schultz, 1993). Quality education is thus linked to human capital development and educational performance (Barro & Lee, 2000; Livingstone, 1997; Watkins, et al., 2001) . However, understanding the enormous resource disparities that exist among most countries of the world, creating equal opportunities for members of the disadvantaged groups and enabling them gain access to quality education is a dream that is currently unachievable in most developing countries (UNESCO, 2003b; Watkins, et al., 2001). Hundreds of millions of the world's children remain out of school (CIDA, 2002). According to the World Bank, one out of every five children aged between 6-12 years in developing countries, an estimated 113 million children are out of school. Forty percent of the out-of-school population resides in Sub Saharan Africa, forty percent in South Asia, and over fifteen per cent in the Middle East and North Africa. Sixty percent of these are girls. One child in every four drops out of school without completing five years of basic education (World Bank, 2001, p. 5).

Certainly, millions of these children drop out of school as a result of the poor quality of educational services offered by many countries' education systems (Atchoarena & Hite, 2001; Gyimah-Brempong, 2003). In most cases, dropping out of school is a consequence of dwindling public resources earmarked for education.

Defining Quality of Education

While quality of education is an important concept commonly referred to by many, it does not seem to have a definition that is universally recognized and accepted (Kellaghan & Greaney, 2001; Ross & Mahlck, 1990; Welch, 2000). Most educators define quality of education basing on learners' examination results obtained in individual schools, teacher/pupil ratio, availability of educational resource-inputs, and other considerations (Atchoarena & Hite, 2001). Thus most scholars have conceptualized the definition of quality of education in terms of resource-inputs and performance. Jimenez and Pinzon (1999) define quality of education as "a dynamic concept that focuses on capacity and performance of the education systems and of its schools" (p. 4). The term dynamic connotes that quality of education is "constantly changing to adapt to a world whose societies are undergoing profound social and economic transformation" (UNESCO, 2003b, p. 1).

In the context of this ever changing world and its equally changing needs, Makwati et al (2003) contend that perceiving quality in education as universally understood and defined is no longer acceptable and valid. Quality of education, therefore, has become more "country or environment specific and related to the goals, expectations and aspirations of a given community, and these may change over time" (Makwati, et al., 2003, p. 10). Such changes create a situation whereby "access to technology, modern education, and resources play a major role in the ability to contribute or adapt to change" (UNESCO, 2003b, p. 1). The available resources deployed and the extent to which these resources-inputs are efficiently and effectively used becomes substantially vital in determining the quality of education (Gyimah-Brempong, 2003; Psacharopoulos, 2000; Stuart, 1994). All these resource inputs may profoundly influence the kind and quality of the educational services offered as being either of acceptable or unacceptable standards to the citizens of a given country or country-specific context (Cleland, 1994; Makwati, et al., 2003; Welch, 2000).

Nevertheless, even though notions of quality must be context specific, it is possible to cautiously use a broad formulaic construction to understand quality in general. Building on Ramecker's (2001) ideas, many current research projects conceptualize quality of education as:

(EQ = Education Quality, A = Access, E = Efficiency, Effectiveness)

Figure 1.1 shows that the greater the overlap between access, efficiency and effectiveness of resource inputs, the better the educational quality. Conceptually, a perfect overlap would mean absolute educational quality made available for all citizens of a nation.

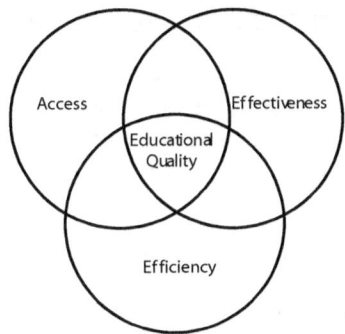

Figure 1.1 Conceptualization of Educational Quality

The challenge facing most governments is how to strike a balance (maximizing the overlap) amongst the three key components of educational quality: access, efficiency, and effectiveness (Levacic & Glover, 1997). Given the current realization of the influence of unavoidably embedded, context-specific issues, it is not surprising that the quality of education is declining in most education systems. This issue of decline in quality of education is addressed in the following section.

Declining Quality of Education

The quality of a nation's education system is the foundation to her social and economic growth (CIDA, 2002; Lockheed, et al., 1991; UNESCO, 2001). All stakeholders in education are increasingly attaching greater value to the quality of education. Unfortunately, the diminishing national resources and the lack of critical resources undermine the quality of educational opportunities, particularly in developing countries (Anderson, 2002; Atchoarena & Hite, 2001; Kellaghan & Greaney, 1992; Rameckers, 2001). This declining quality of education has become an issue of great concern to most governments of the world (Chapman & Mahlck, 1993; Mùgimu & Hite, 2001), since, quality education is fundamental in contributing to educational effectiveness and to the success of individuals, families, communities, and nations.

Unfortunately, majority of the disadvantaged youth, predominantly girls, in the world are less likely to gain access to quality education. Indeed, while most governments are striving to increase schooling opportunities for their disadvantaged youth at all levels, they may not realize that "it is one thing to enroll and keep children in school; and what they learn is another matter." Students in many developing countries frequently go through their education systems without actually learning valuable basic skills that are crucial and critical for their future survival. The major reason is that the schools these students attend lack the basic resources needed for effective students' learning outcomes. However, for over a half a century, numerous educational effectiveness studies have examined the impact of school resources on school outcomes (Cohen, Raudenbush, & Ball, 2003; Gannicott & Throsby, 1998). Therefore, the rest of this chapter is devoted to an overview of Educational Effectiveness research.

EDUCATIONAL EFFECTIVENESS STUDIES AND SCHOOL RESOURCES

> How can schools. ... manage to implement the centrally stated policies successfully if they are not provided with the proper conditions and a just amount of resources? (Bosker, Creemers, & Stringfield, 1999).

For centuries, educators and policy makers have maintained that the quality and quantity of school resources available to schools make the largest difference in students' academic achievement (Firestone, 1991b; Marion & Flanigan, 2001; Reynolds, 1990). However, the full range of empirical evidence on this important point is inconclusive and controversial. For example, James Coleman's influential study in the United States on the equality of educational opportunity explored the role of schooling in relation to performance outcomes in basic skills of students of various social classes and racial groups. Coleman et al.(1966) found that socio-economic status (SES) and family background accounted for the largest portion in students' outcomes. As a result of Coleman's study and many subsequent studies, educationists typically concluded that the relative impact of school resources is far less important to students' academic achievement than previously thought (Jencks, et al., 1972a; Mayeske, Okada, Beaton, Cohen, & Wisler, 1973).

But, some recent studies seem to suggest that schools and resources could make a substantial difference in students' outcomes and educational effectiveness to a larger degree than previously shown or suggested by Coleman in 1966 (Card & Krueger, 2000; Reynolds, 1994; Taylor, Pearson, Clark, & Walpole, 2000; Townsend, 1997). Furthermore, research in developing countries indicates that in deprived conditions the influence of school resources on student outcomes is more pronounced than in industrialized countries (Fuller & Clarke, 1994; Fuller & Heyneman, 1989; Harbison & Hanushek, 1992; Heyneman & Loxley, 1983; Scheerens, 2001a, 2001b, 2002; Teddlie, 2003). However, these research efforts in developing countries predominantly focus on primary schools, while very few studies look at secondary schools (Figueredo & Anzolone, 2003; Fuller & Clarke, 1994; Scheerens, 2001b; Wyatt, 1996).

Whether additional school resources, per se, make a difference to student performance remains controversial and unclear (J. W. Lee & Barro, 1997; Ludwig & Bassi, 1999; Wobmann, 2000). To investigate what school factors and resources actually account for school performance and contribute to the improvement of quality of education, Educational Effectiveness (EE) researchers have used various performance indicators as proxies for quality of education (Herpen, 1992; J. W. Lee & Barro, 1997; Scheerens, 1991). Typical performance indicators include such items as standardized test scores; school attendance rates; school dropout rates; stakeholders' participation; infrastructure; administration; teacher training; and expenditure per student (Creemers, 1996; Hanushek, 1995; L. J. P. Jimenez & Pinzon, 1999; Rameckers, 2001). While research in developing countries in this regard on primary education is extensive, albeit controversial, very little is known about the impact of school resources on school performance at the secondary school level in developing countries. Therefore, the quest to identify what critical resources actually contribute to a secondary school's ability to accomplish critical goals and objectives in education is central to this project.

The vast literature base of EE research has offered a potential wealth of important knowledge to guide and influence policy decisions in education, relative to the central antecedents of educational quality. Yet, numerous researchers have criticized this literature for various purported methodological, theoretical, and practical weaknesses--especially for their over-reliance on the production function models (Bliss, 1991; Cohn, Millman, & Chew, 1975; Gannicott & Throsby, 1998; Monk & Plecki, 1999; Richards, 1991a; Scheerens, 1991). While the issues of more or less appropriate research methodologies will be addressed later in this chapter, an important consideration is the role and usefulness of the currently existing EE studies in the industrialized and developing regions of the world.

EE STUDIES IN INDUSTRIALIZED COUNTRIES

Overall conclusions regarding the body of EE studies in industrialized countries indicate that the impact of resource-inputs factors on school performance is fairly small (ADEA, 2003; Monk & Plecki, 1999; Scheerens, 2000). The origins of EE research can be traced to the early 1960s and 70s in large-scale studies commissioned by the congress such as Coleman (1966) and Jenks (1972b).

The Coleman Report

In the early 1960s, majority of American children attended schools that were largely unequal and segregated, irrespective of the desegregation decision of 1954 (Brown v. Board of Education) where the U.S. Supreme Court held that separate schools for Negro and White children were inherently unequal (Yudof, Levin, Moran, & Kirp, 2002) and therefore unconstitutional. In the spirit of identifying ways to discourage segregation, Coleman's study investigated the lack of availability of equal educational opportunities for individuals from low-income and minority groups. Coleman's study surveyed approximately 645,000 pupils in more than 2,883 schools around United States. The findings of this study indicated that the family and socio-economic status of the child contributed more to predicting the variance in student achievement than traditional school characteristics such as expenditure per pupil, quantity of instructional materials, and others (Coleman, et al., 1966). Randall, Cooper, & Hite (1999) suggest that the impact of the Coleman study on racial segregation and integration of minority students was remarkable because the report's findings stimulated extensive critiques and fundamentally influenced future educational research and policy agenda up to this day.

Related Studies

Findings by Jencks et al.(1972b), in a subsequent study, were close to those of Coleman. In their study, they utilized data collected in a national survey comprising variables that addressed a wide range of policy issues related to schooling and inequality. These researchers found that "family background explained nearly half of the variation while traditional indicators of educational attainment only explained about two percent of the variation in students' educational attainment between schools of very different conditions" (Jencks, et al., 1972b, p. 143). Mayeske et al.(1973) conducted research that also built on Coleman's work and found about 85 percent of the variation in average achievement between schools to be associated with family background characteristics.

Findngs of these early large-scale studies in the '60s and '70s were heartbreaking to many policy makers and educators, especially those who strongly believed that schools and school resources really made a difference (Picus, 1997; Scheerens & Bosker, 1997). Richards (1991a) indicates that many researchers and stakeholders in education misinterpreted these findings to suggest that school resources did not matter at all in influencing the life chances of low-income and minority youth. Bliss (1991), for instance, wrote that the "Coleman findings were devastating" ...[and therefore] "practitioners, and scholars of education alike have sought reassurance that schools can make an important difference, beyond the effect of home background" (p. 53-54). Furthermore, simply suggesting that educational achievement depended on the family, not what schools did or could do, as proposed by Coleman et al., (1966) and other subsequent studies, undermined the "basic beliefs about the legitimacy of the educational enterprise and the efficacy of educators" (Firestone, 1991a, p. 21). Indeed, many stakeholders in education widely accepted that at the time of the study, "the findings of the Coleman report shook the very foundations of core beliefs about equity, resources, and opportunity" (Galvin, 1999, p. 132) and continue to this day. As indicated by Bliss (1991), the early studies ignited further research in the '80s and '90s to search for the "truths" that could help to overturn Coleman's findings.

Studies Diverging from Coleman's and other Related Studies

The notion that family background and not schooling accounted for most differences in student achievement was highly contested and became the primary motivation of the Educational Effectiveness (EE) research movement (Scheerens, 1999; Scheerens & Bosker, 1997). Donald Edmonds (1979), on his part, rejected the idea that schools do not matter, partly because he recognized many schools that existed and were successful in teaching basic skills to all children. He contended, "all children are eminently educable. ... When schools choose to do so" (Edmonds, 1979, p. 20-21). Edmonds' notion has been taken to mean that all children can learn, if and only if, schools focus their energies and resources on their needs (Brock, 2002; Lawton, 1994). Edmonds strongly believed that school resources are important components of effective schools and that school resources are fundamentally important for student achievement.

Aim (1972) examined the relationships between socio-economic status (SES) and the availabilities of educational resources and the relationship between educational resources and educational outcomes. He utilized four standardized achievement tests and retention rate as proxies for educational outcomes. His sample comprised 94 school districts containing 149 secondary schools. He found a statistically significant relationship between SES and resource input measures. He also found that schools in higher SES areas tended to provide their students with greater amounts of educational resources and these resources were related to student achievement. Rutter et al (1979) conducted a study focusing on secondary schools in London examining whether schools and teachers had an impact on the development of the children under their care. These authors found that schools impacted on children's development and that it mattered what school the child attended (Rutter, et al., 1979).

In recent years a shift in position from Coleman and his colleagues can be seen regarding the role of schools in students' achievement. While Coleman (up to his death in 1995) and his colleagues (2000) maintain that socio-economic background of the students remained important in the achievement of students, differences between schools and school resources are also important in explaining the differences in student achievement. These authors further contended that differences in schools and school facilities, curriculum, and teachers seem to have more effect on the achievement of minority students than achievement of other students. For instance, Coleman et al., (2000) reported that 20 percent of the achievement of Negroes in the south is associated with particular schools they go to compared to only 10 percent of the achievement of whites in the south (p. 163). These findings are consistent with what Rutter et al. (1979) found. Specifically, Coleman, and Rutter et al. would agree in more recent years that what school a child attended mattered significantly.

Furthermore, differences in school and teacher quality seem to deeply affect achievement of the most disadvantaged students (Coleman, et al., 2000). Jencks et al. (2000) found that cumulative impact of school quality alters the average student's educational attainment in less than half a year [and that] attending the right school may...make an enormous difference to particular students (p. 173). However, one interesting paradox is that the kind of school that might be most effective for one student may not be so for another student (Jencks, et al., 2000). This factor has the potential to confound our understanding about the differential impact of school resources on students' educational achievement and school performance in general.

Nevertheless, these early EE studies could not clearly and concretely explain the relationship between school resources and school performance, because these studies showed some ambiguity and lacked agreement on different educational indicators. For instance, Rutter (1983) indicated that a few schools [showed] superior performance on some measures but inferior outcomes on others (p. 8). Therefore, the relationships between school resources and school performance remained and still remain obscure, which led to further EE research. The following section discusses some of the recent relevant EE studies.

Recent Studies in Industrialized Countries

With the profound advancement in technology and computer software, many researchers have increasingly assumed that recent EE studies should hold greater promise in providing better information on the impact of school resources and school performance (Richards, 1991a). Shive (2000) utilized hierarchical linear multiple-level modeling techniques on longitudinal data (collected from public elementary schools in the USA) to examine the relationships between school resources and aggregated student outcomes. His findings are mixed. He found teacher education and experience to be statistically significant predictors of student performance on standardized test scores in Reading and Mathematics. Shive (2000) also found that per-pupil spending from the local sources was not significant in any of his models. Therefore, his findings are consistent with earlier studies in industrialized countries (Hanushek, 1989, 1995, 1996, 1997).

Wobmann (2000), another researcher, studied more than 260,000 students from 39 countries and concluded that the international differences in student performance are not caused by differences in schooling resources but mainly by differences in educational institutions. However, his study did not explain how schools are different. His findings therefore are rather controversial. For instance, he reported that equipments and instructional materials and teachers' experience and education are positive predictors to school outcomes (Wobmann, 2000, p. 52).

A meta-analytical study on teacher characteristics and student achievement concluded that students learn better from teachers with certain characteristics. Indeed, "high school students clearly learn more from teachers with certification in Mathematics, degrees related to Mathematics, and coursework related to Mathematics" (Wayne & Youngs, 2003 , p. 107).

Card and Kruger (2000) studied data from 1900-1959 on school resource differences between whites and blacks in North and South Carolina. They concluded that perhaps the strongest evidence that resources matter comes from the analysis of the vast differences in resources for blacks and whites who attended schools in the segregated state (p. 101). These researchers reported that the payoff to each year of education was greater for individuals who were from states that devoted more resources to education. Furthermore, levels of earning and educational attainment were positively associated with school resources (Card & Krueger, 2000 , p. 101). Obviously, these conclusions should be considered in light of the social, cultural, political, and economic influences of that era in American history, as these critical issues would impact and interact with the basic resource data. The researchers, however, did little in this respect. This potential critical flaw in the analytical framework of Card and Krueger casts serious doubt on the validity of their claims. Given the likely variations in terms of prevailing conditions under which these resources were allocated from 1900 to 1959, it becomes problematic to isolate effects of resources from other social, cultural, political and economic factors.

Additionally, Leaver (2003) examined the effects of public high school resources on the performance of college and beyond students and found that expenditure per pupil has statistically significant positive effects on SAT performance. This finding is contrary to what Shive (2000) found. Leaver also reported that high school resources seem to have only bare minimal effect on the average SAT scores in the schools that the college and beyond sampled students attended. Unlike Shive (2000), Leaver found teacher/student coefficient to be negative for each group of schools and statistically insignificant at five percent significance level. Leaver concluded that his study did not support the notion that measurable school resources had a large impact on the students' performance in the college and beyond sample.

Nevertheless, Leaver was careful to qualify his conclusion by acknowledging the limitations of his data sets. He argued that his data sets were not specifically designed for the analysis of change in school resources or student performance over time (Leaver, 2003). Shive (2000) also presented similar concerns regarding data limitations. The general theme arising from these researchers is that they all seem to acknowledge the underlying methodological and practical limitations related to data quality that could have hindered the researcher's ability to measure the impact of school resources on student performance accurately and reliably (Aim, 1972; Leaver, 2003; Richards, 1991a; Scheerens, 1991; Shive, 2000; Spady, 1976; Spencer & Wiley, 1981). Indeed, measuring and assessing the quality of education is and continues to be problematic. As Ross and Mahlch (1990) put it, "educational inputs and processes are extremely difficult to measure in a reliable and valid manner" (p. 75).

Yet, policy makers and educators increasingly acknowledge the role of less tangible factors that influence the level of educational quality, which are also extremely difficult to measure (Atchoarena & Hite, 2001). These less tangible factors may be confounded with the constructs related to school resources thus obstructing the researcher's ability to make accurate inferences (Cohn, et al., 1975; Ludwig & Bassi, 1999). For instance, taking one vital resource input (teachers), Hanushek (1986) indicated the difficulty that exists in isolating "objectively or subjectively the systematic differences of both backgrounds of teachers and their idiosyncratic choices of teaching style and methods" (p. 1164). The ability to interpret accurately the relationships between educational inputs and educational outcomes is confounded even further, rendering the situation so difficult to know what actually contributes directly, without intervening and potentially confounding influences, educational effectiveness. The following section discusses educational effectiveness studies in developing countries.

EE STUDIES IN DEVELOPING COUNTRIES

> The third world families and educators have much to teach the North Americans about how to make schools more effective when resources are abysmally scarce. In the U.S. when school quality is low, educators often argue that more money is the best remedy. In contrast, third world families' earnest commitment to education and teachers' extraordinary efforts persist even in the face of material poverty. The richness of this deep motivation and social cohesion, so evident in third world schools, could provide important lessons for American educators
> (Fuller & Heyneman, 1989, p. 18).

Evidently, research efforts on EE studies in developing countries lags behind that of the United States and other industrialized countries (Wobmann, 2001). However, many of the international studies available challenge Coleman's findings that quality and quantity of school resources make the greatest difference in school performance, especially in conditions where resources are abysmally scarce (Fuller & Clarke, 1994; Fuller & Heyneman, 1989; Hanushek & Luque, 2002; Harbison & Hanushek, 1992; Heyneman & Loxley, 1983; Scheerens, 1999, 2001a, 2001b; Teddlie, 2003).

Table 1.1, clearly reveals that a higher percentage of studies report more significant positive associations of resource inputs in the developing countries than industrialized countries. According to Scheerens (1999, 2001b), the greater impact of resources on performance in developing countries could be due to the larger resource gaps and variations in the developing countries relative to their counterparts in the industrialized countries. If this is the case, or even plausibly so, this would create the need for more research within the developing country context to establish the differential impact between industrialized and developing contexts (Scheerens, 2000, 2001b). Furthermore, Caillods and Postlethwaite (1995, p. 13) reported that "between-school-differences can account for over 30 percent of pupils' differences at grade 6, 50 percent at grade 9, and 60 -70 percent at grade 12 in the developing countries." EE studies in developing countries have focused mainly on examining "how to provide the best education for all with limited resources" (Riddell, 1997, p. 187). Therefore, policies focusing on improving the quality and quantity of school resources are not only urgently needed but vital in the developing countries (Fuller & Clarke, 1994).

Unfortunately, in most developing countries primary school level EE studies predominate, and extremely few studies have looked at secondary school level. Thus, an even greater need exists for further EE research at secondary school level. Harbers & Davies (1997) contended that much of the EE studies research is patterned on that of industrialized countries. Yet, this approach has potential serious flaws since many factors are context-specific and therefore different in industrialized and developing countries (Lloyd, Tawila, Clark, & Mensch, 2003; Scheerens, 2001b). This notion of existing contextual-specificity and its realities in the education of many children in developing countries is supported by a recent South African study (Harber & Muthukrishna, 2000).

Table 1.1

Percentage of Studies With Positive Association of Resource Input Variables and Achievement for Industrialized as Compared to Developing Countries

Input	Industrialized countries significant positive association (%)	Developing countries significant positive association (%)
Teacher-pupil ratio	15	27
Teacher's education	9	55
Teacher's experience	29	35
Teacher's salary	20	30
Per pupil expenditure	27	50

Source: Scheerens (2001b, p. 362) as extracted from (Hanushek, 1995, 1997)

The reason for attaching some importance to this study is the fact that the authors utilized qualitative methods, such as observational approaches to examine school and classroom instructional processes in three schools with very different social and political contextual backgrounds.

Note that, qualitative methods are currently the preferred approaches in the contemporary EE research in the developing world (Fertig, 2000; Scheerens, 2001b). Harber and Muthukrishna (2000) through qualitative techniques demonstrated the difficulties in judging schools in one context using criteria developed in another. Nevertheless, many EE studies are grounded in the assumption that what works for one country or region works for all (ADEA, 2003; UNESCO, 2001), which assumption is apparently proving more and more frequently to be a fallacy.

LIMITATIONS OF EE IN DEVELOPING COUNTRIES

Many scholars have criticized EE studies for their methodological, theoretical, and practical limitations (Heyneman & Loxley, 1983; J. W. Lee & Barro, 1997; Scheerens, 1999; M. D. Young, 1999). One of the key limitations is lack of reliable and valid data (Chapman & Mahlck, 1993; Hanushek, 1997; Tsang, 2002). Other methodological weaknesses highlighted in the current EE literature include: (i) the use of small samples; (ii) insufficient adjustment for important background characteristics of schooling; (iii) reactive research arrangements; and, (iv) improper use of analysis techniques (Ralph & Fennessey, 1983; Scheerens, 1991, 1992). Hanushek (2003) also contended that the practice of using common instruments to assess education quality across industrialized and developing countries—could lead to potential research problems. Even when efforts are made to adapt the instruments to the local conditions, some of the items may still remain irrelevant (Nassor & Mohammed, 1998; Nkamba & Kanyika, 1998). Indeed, given the existing broad diversity and variations in terms of school structure, curriculum, language, culture, etc between industrialized and developing countries, the common practice of generating and interpreting data from the global assessment studies is potentially problematic (Barro & Lee, 2000; Fuller & Clarke, 1994; Hanushek, 2003b; Heyneman & Loxley, 1983; J. W. Lee & Barro, 1997)--because it is like comparing mangoes with oranges.

To illustrate this point it could be useful to consider a study by Heyneman and Loxley (1982), which focused on the school quality factor (i.e. teacher quality) influences on academic achievement across twenty-nine high- and low- income countries. These authors reported that when they analyzed data for individual countries separately, they found huge differences between the countries. They found that the number of statistically influential variables on student achievement almost doubled. That is, in addition to the original ten variables that emerged when aggregating all of the countries together, when these countries were treated separately there were 19 statistically influential variables in India; 19 variables in Chile; and 18 variables in Germany (Heyneman & Loxley, 1982). In the disaggregated analyses the authors also reported a significant increase in the variance explained by school effects, and the increase tended to be greatest in the poorer countries. These highlighted methodological, theoretical, and practical limitations that continue to undermine the quality, accuracy, validity, and usability of EE findings across and between industrialized and developing contexts.The following sub-sections present relevant literature that examines the impact of physical, financial, and human resources on primary and secondary school or student performance. Attention will be focused on issues between developed and developing country contexts.

PHYSICAL RESOURCES

The quest to understand the relationship between physical resources and school performance remains unclear. A meta-analytical study by McGuffey (1982) indicated that a schools' physical environment impacts student performance. Most of the studies included by McGuffey looked at facilities, pupil's self-concept, ages of school buildings, and other educational resource variables thought to impact pupil achievement. Majority of the studies showed that school building ages were significantly related to student achievement. McGuffey's findings seem to support the notion that educational facilities are important in facilitating teaching and learning processes (McGuffey, 1982). Yet in the developing countries, there is a prevalent shortage of educational facilities. For instance, Mutakyahwa (1999) reports the lack of critical teaching facilities in Tanzanian secondary schools. This situation is likely to be similar in many other developing countries. Fuller & Clarke (1994, p. 137) indicated that the distance to school, the quality of facilities, and the presence of basic instructional tools could attract parents and students to particular schools as well as influence their performance once there. In fact, "the quality of the facilities influences which teachers and children attend a particular school" (Murnane, 1981, p. 25). However, Mingat (2003) observed, "It is what goes on in the classroom that accounts, more than the physical packaging in which educational services are provided" (p. 26). Mingat's assertion may be true and acceptable in the context of industrialized countries where most schools, at least, have a relatively homogeneous distribution of the basic facilities and resources they need. This notion may not be true and acceptable in the context of developing countries, where a wide range of variation in distribution of physical resources exists among schools (Inkeles, 1979; Rutter, 1983).

It is widely recognized that majority of the schools in developing countries lack even the basic resources and facilities needed to achieve their minimal objectives (Anderson, 2002; Kulpoo, 1998; Nassor & Mohammed, 1998; Nkamba & Kanyika, 1998). Furthermore, a study on the impact of educational quality on school exit conducted in Egypt revealed that, "girls are less likely to exit when they attend schools with better physical facilities" (Lloyd, et al., 2003). Apparently whether or not physical resources influence school performance in developing countries remains a difficult issue to resolve. Certainly, a serious question exists regarding whether use of data from industrialized contexts to generalize about those in developing areas of the world is viable and useful.

Staff Accommodation

No empirical studies we know of have investigated the relationship between school performance and staff housing per se. Yet staff housing remains an important challenge to most schools and education systems in developing countries. In addition, in most developing countries, staff housing is a financial responsibility of the employing school. Certainly, housing in rural areas for teachers and administrators is especially difficult to find. Since the hiring and retaining of teachers in developing countries is considered a basic part of their employment contract, this challenge ends up contributing to reluctance of qualified teachers to teach and remain in rural schools. Thus, rural schools find it extreme difficulty to attract and to keep the best qualified teachers (Caillods & Postlethwaite, 1995; Hallak, 1990; Warwick & Jatoi, 1994). Whether providing decent housing for teachers and school administrators translates into better educational quality and better educational services offered to students is not clear. First, living in good housing near the school where they work, apparently would help teachers and administrators to become more accessible and available to assume the additional responsibilities needed to serve the educational needs of the students better. Given that good local housing would positively impact student performance. Then, providing good staff housing locally would reduce the costs of transporting school staff, making available significant additional financial resources for other vital educational programs, hence improving student performance. Neither of these issues, however, has received any significant treatment in the current research literature, and therefore both remain only speculative.

Instructional Materials and Textbooks

In developing countries, textbooks and other instructional material were found to be consistently important to student performance (Fuller & Heyneman, 1989; Hanushek, 1995; Mingat, 2003). Yet, teachers lack teaching aids and instructional materials (BB) [black boards], textbooks, science equipments in secondary education. Schools and classrooms are not always adequate in terms of lighting, ventilation, furniture, sanitation facilities, availability of drinking water etc" (Caillods & Postlethwaite, 1995, p. 6).

Empirical evidence suggests that in impoverished conditions the availability of basic school resources such as textbooks, classrooms and trained teachers are fundamental to student performance (Hanushek, 1995; Harbison & Hanushek, 1992; M. E. Lockheed & E. A. Hanushek, 1988; Lockheed & Levin, 1993). Caillods & Hallak (1995) reported that shortage of books and instructional materials constrained the achievement of students in their study. A Zimbabwean study of Nyagura & Riddell (1993) revealed that advantaged schools in terms of resources such as textbooks, and other instructional materials performed better than other schools without such resources. Woessmann (2001) reported students attending schools with adequate instructional materials scored 7 points higher in Mathematics and Science relative to students attending schools with inadequate instructional materials. Furthermore, "students in schools with a great shortage of materials scored 6 points worse in Mathematics and 12 points in Science" (Woessmann, 2001, p. 70).

In developing countries the lions' share of funding goes to teachers' salaries (Gannicott & Throsby, 1998; Gyimah-Brempong, 2003; Voigts, 1998), resulting in very little being actually spent on textbooks and other instructional materials. For instance, many developing countries spend under $4 per child per year on the purchase of instructional materials, and increasingly parents are shouldering more costs in procuring stationary and books for their children (Caillods & Postlethwaite, 1995). Nonetheless, textbooks and other instruction materials must be utilized in order to make a difference (Harris & Dzinyela, 1997; Kulpoo, 1998; Machingaidze, Pfukani, & Shumba, 1998). In some instances, however, even though resources are available they are sometimes not used. For example, Schubert and Prouty-Harris (2003) indicates that:

> In Ghana, ...although the textbooks had been delivered
> to the schools, only a few of the books had made it to
> the classroom and in the hands of pupils. Most textbooks
> were stored safely in a cabinet because teachers feared
> they would be held accountable for damage to the books
> (p. 27-28).

As indicated by Schubert and Prouty-Harris (2003), simply counting the number of instructional materials and resources available in schools may not reveal much because, although the materials are in place, they might not even be used. Therefore, ensuring that proper instructional materials and facilities are not only made available, but also are used to facilitate student outcomes becomes vital (Woessmann, 2001). Doing so is an efficient and effective way of using available limited resources, the World Bank (1995) stated, "the effective use of textbooks must involve training teachers in the use of the new books and providing teachers guides" (p. 86).

Class size

The actual impact of class size in developing countries remains equivocal. Hanushek (1995) reports that class size was found to be statistically insignificant in relation to student performance in both industrialized countries and developing countries. Lee & Barro (1997) reported a strong correlation between pupil-teacher ratio and superior student performance. They suggest that smaller class sizes contribute more to higher student performance. Willms and Somers (2001) also found the coefficient of pupil-teacher ratio to be negative, suggesting that achievement scores decline with increasing class size (p. 434). Furthermore, some empirical evidence that "class sizes might influence teacher productivity" (Cohn, et al., 1975, p. 20). Lee & Barro (1997) claimed that "pupil-teacher ratio is expected to be negatively correlated with test scores because students learn more rapidly by having more frequent interactions with teachers in smaller classes" (p. 6).

Conversely, a number of other studies have claimed that there is little evidence that smaller class sizes are better than larger classes (Caillods & Postlethwaite, 1995; Card & Krueger, 2000; Hanushek, 1995; Monk & Plecki, 1999). Wobmann (2000) found a statistically significant positive relationship between class size and student performance. The issue of class size in developing context is further confounded when effects of efficiency are introduced. For example, Wobmann (2000) indicated that "Test scores in Mathematics and Science were higher in education systems with larger classes,, resources are more effectively used in countries with larger classes" (p. 76). To further cloud this picture, this claim by Wobmann stands directly opposed to those by Lee & Barro (1997). These authors made the claim that students attending large classes often tend to be unruly in such settings while their teachers tend to focus more on rote learning, rather than on problem-solving skills (J. W. Lee & Barro, 1997).

Nonetheless, class size remains a persistent and therefore an important policy issue. Studies in industrialized countries show that costs are likely to rise as a result of the need to construct additional classrooms and to recruit additional teachers (Brewer, Krop, Gill, & Reichardt, 1999; Gannicott & Throsby, 1998; Odden & Archibald, 2001). Indeed, reducing class size has unintended consequences. Dennison (1990, p. 63) reported, "...All other things being equal, a decrease of one pupil in a class of twenty adds five per cent to spending on teachers' salaries ... [that may involve] several millions of pounds".

Incidentally, "higher spending and small class sizes seem to correspond to inferior mathematics and science results, though the effect is relatively small" (Woessmann, 2001, p. 70). This notion is consistent in light of policies related to class size reduction that tend to push for additional spending of financial resources to create additional classrooms and hire extra teachers instead of redistributing additional financial resources on core educational programs that directly contribute to student learning (Picus, 1997; Rutter, 1980; Wobmann, 2001). Thus, class size reduction would negatively impact student performance.

Understanding that class sizes are typically several times larger in developing countries than in industrialized countries (Anderson, 2002; Harber & Davies, 1997; Mingat, 2003), becomes unclear whether class size actually does matter in school performance in the developing countries. Therefore, whether class size of secondary

Chapter 1 - Preamble: School Resources, Educational Quality & Effectivenes

schools in the context of the developing countries may or may not account for school performance is yet to be authoritatively clarified.

School size

Similar to class size, empirical evidences on relationship between school size and school performance remains inconclusive at best. Some studies have suggested that smaller schools are more effective (V. E. Lee, 1997). Other studies suggest that larger schools are better and more effective (Monk & Plecki, 1999; Silins & Murray-Harvey, 1999). Both camps present pros and cons for each size of schools. The prominent work done by Reynolds (1990) indicates that, at least in Europe, school size affects pupil performance. That is, "eight percent of the variance in pupil's examination attainment is school related" (p. 12).

Evidence shows economies of a scale to be associated with the size of the school, it usually becomes cheaper to operate a larger school than a small school (Liang, 2002; Monk & Plecki, 1999; Sanders, 2002b). Caillods & Lewin (2001) reported secondary school enrolments much below 1000, are associated with increasing costs, and that above this level cost per student fall slowly until they reach a plateau. This is, however, a measure of school efficiency, and not necessarily one of effectiveness. Simply because a school being more efficient in using resources does not mean that it will be more effective in delivering higher student performance.

In the end, the evidence on the impact of school size on school performance and quality is mixed and inconclusive (Monk & Plecki, 1999; Rutter, 1980, 1983). In addition, studies on the impact of school size on school performance in the context of developing countries are extremely rare. Whether school size is an important predictor of school performance in secondary schools of the developing countries remains to be demonstrated.

Science Laboratory

Most governments in developing countries perceive science teaching as the panacea to producing quality education, national economic development, and of course, future scientists (Thulstrup, 1999; WorldBank, 1995). "Science laboratories hold enormous status in third world [developing countries] secondary schools, yet they do not seem to consistently boost student achievement and may not be relevant in teaching basic scientific concepts" (Fuller & Heyneman, 1989, p. 17). Nonetheless, national ministries tend to invest substantially on science laboratory construction and science teaching in schools. Considering that science laboratory construction and education is very costly, the consequent returns on the investment to school performance may not be justifiable (K. M. Lewin, 2000; Thulstrup, 1999; WorldBank, 1995). So far no empirical evidence has indicated that availability of school laboratories in schools contributes significantly to school performance in secondary schools (K. M. Lewin, 2000; Ware, 1999). Case and Deaton (1999) found a statistical significant negative effect of primary and secondary science laboratories on literacy test scores.

Furthermore, the possession of a science laboratory in a school is one thing, but actually utilizing that laboratory to boost student achievement is another. Realizing that utilization of science laboratories may depend heavily upon factors such as willingness and competence of teachers to use its facilities is extremely important. Given that even when science laboratories may be available, they are quite often not utilized at all, let alone efficiently and effectively. Consequently, students are often tested on laboratory work that they were not taught (K. M. Lewin & Gunne, 2000; Ware, 1992b), and they usually perform poorly. This view may be a possible explanation for negative statistical associations of science laboratories to student performance. Whether secondary schools with more access to adequately furnished science laboratories outperform other schools, is yet another critical area that needs to be carefully investigated.

School Library

Do libraries contribute to school performance? Of all the resource issues that have attained prominence in school and student performance research, the library has been consistently affirmed in that it rests almost uncontested in most contemporary literature. "Libraries can be looked at as important cultural niche in the provision of knowledge and information" (Mann, 2001, p. 9). Indeed, virtually all scholars in this area agree that school libraries do impact on school performance and student achievement (Lonsdale, 2003; Scheerens, 2001a). Lonsdale (2003) reviewed studies that examined the impact of school libraries on student achievement. Overall, the vast majority of these studies indicated that school libraries could have positive impact on student performance and test scores are often higher when there is higher usage of the library (Lance, 2002; Lonsdale, 2003; Williams, Coles, & Wavell, 2002). Case and Denton (1999) studied school inputs and educational outcomes in South Africa and also reported a significant positive influence of secondary school library on literacy test scores. Fuller (1987) indicated that 15 out of 18 studies reviewed found school libraries to have statistical significant influence on pupil achievement in developing countries.

Additionally, a library comprises many educational resources held by a school outside the classroom. These school library provisions can facilitate, among other things, self-directed learning (Harber & Davies, 1997). Empirical evidence shows that "libraries can make a positive difference to students' self-esteem, confidence, independence and sense of responsibility with regard to their own learning" (Lonsdale, 2003, p. 1). In developing countries, shortage of library facilities is evident, particularly in secondary schools. This shortage curtails the quality of education (Liang, 2002). Yet, adequate school library provisions could even make much more impact on student performance. Given that schools in developing countries are often comprised of large and overcrowded classrooms, poorly trained teachers, and a lack of basic instructional materials. Availability of well-furnished school libraries could compensate for some of these limitations and could also facilitate quality and equity of education in developing countries (S. Lee, Brown, Mekis, & Singh, 2003).

However, some researchers have asserted that the availability of a school library is not enough if the facilities are not used (Kulpoo, 1998). For instance, S. Lee et al., (2003) indicated that in Malaysia "while libraries exist in every school, their role is secondary because rote learning of specific subject matter is more important in performance in examinations. The education system places heavy emphasis on success in examinations" (p. 4). As such, in Malaysia, they do not utilize the school library facilities effectively and efficiently, as they ought to. To include availability and usability of school libraries as constructs in research studies examining the influence of libraries in secondary school student performance is imperative. Nonetheless, most of the research done has focused on primary school levels rather than secondary school levels (Lonsdale, 2003). Moreover, empirical evidence seems to suggest that the influence of school libraries diminishes in upper secondary school levels (Fuller & Clarke, 1994; Lonsdale, 2003). This underscores the need to examine the influence of school libraries on student performance at secondary school level in developing countries.

FINANCIAL RESOURCES

Are financial resources vital in contributing to school performance? "Insufficient financial resources are often cited as a root cause for the poor quality of education" (CIDA, 2002). Most stakeholders in education readily believe that adding more money to schools will improve the quality of education and consequently school performance.

However, production function studies in both industrialized and developing countries have produced findings that are inconsistent and mixed. Hanushek (1995) reported that in 12 studies on per pupil expenditures in developing countries, half were statistically significant, and the other half were found to be statistically insignificant. Furthermore, Hanushek's numerous meta-analytical studies revealed that there is apparently no systematic relationship between school resources and school performance in industrialized countries (Hanushek, 1981, 1989, 1997, 2003a; Hanushek, Rivkin, & Taylor, 1996).

But many other scholars highly contest Hanushek's findings basing on methodological grounds (Greenwald, Hedges, & Laine, 1996; Hedges, Laine, & Greenwald, 1994; Marion & Flanigan, 2001; Spencer & Wiley, 1981). Critics claim that the vote counting technique used by Hanushek was inadequate. When Hedges, Laine, and Greenward re-analyzed the same data that Hanushek (1986) used in his own analysis, with different methods, they got contradicting results. In their re-analysis, Hedges and colleagues found a systematic positive relationship between school resources and school outcomes (Hedges, et al., 1994; Marion & Flanigan, 2001).

However, in Levin's (1989) view, "Hanushek does not imply that additional spending makes no difference, but that it only makes an apparent difference, on average, in ways that schools presently use additional funding" (p. 16). Furthermore, empirical evidence shows that schools tend to spend on resources that are not directly contributing to students' performance (Hanushek, 1995, 2003a; Picus, 1997). Given the contradictory assertions made by numerous researchers following tremendously vigorous efforts, it is not possible to claim in one way or another that spending more money will necessarily impact education quality and outcomes in industrialized countries (Gannicott & Throsby, 1998; Hanushek, 1989; Wobmann, 2001).

Nonetheless, the possibility that these same expenditures might make a profound difference in developing countries persists, and the debate on financial resources in education remains crucial (Fuller, 1987; Picus, 1997). Whether secondary schools with greater access to more financial resources outperform others is still an issue demanding exploration in the developing context. Therefore, the question to examine the relationships between financial resources and school performance in secondary schools in Mukono, Uganda remains an important one.

HUMAN RESOURCES

> Teachers are a key element in the teaching/learning process and ...constitute in most developing countries the main, if not the only, agent of transmission of knowledge in schools (Caillods & Postlethwaite, 1995, p. 2).

Numerous human resources such as the quality of teachers, principal, students' prior learning ability, and parents have been highlighted by many EE studies to impact school performance. While empirical evidence shows that all these different human resources are important in school performance, determining which of them is most important seems to be unpredictable. Table 1.2 presents a summary on different human resources that seem to be important from the current literature.

In addition, Heyneman and Loxley (1983) examined school and teacher quality available around the world and the impact of those factors on students' achievement in Science. They studied 18 countries comprising a sample of 10,000 schools, 50,000 teachers, and 260,000 students. Heyneman and Loxley found that school and teacher quality in low-income countries explained more than 80 per cent of the variation in student achievement in Science, but less than 28 per cent in industrialized countries. It may seem obvious to assume that the quality of teachers would be more important of these two variables, since teachers directly determine what opportunity students actually have to learn. Irrespective of the guidelines on the curriculum and instructional policies, what actually goes on in the classroom, depends very much upon the teacher's discretion, competence, and interpersonal ability (Suter, 2000; WorldBank, 1994).

Therefore teachers must be motivated to contribute positively towards student learning. In light of all this, the quality of the school principal perhaps becomes extremely vital. A good principal is able to, and should, motivate the teachers to do a good job, without much supervision, to implement and facilitate educational programs that contribute to student outcomes (Senge, 1990; Senge, Kleiner, Roberts, Ross, & Smith, 1994; Sergiovanni, 1984).

Interestingly, Wobmann (2000) found that students taught by female teachers score statistically higher than students taught by male teachers in both Mathematics and Science. This finding is likely influenced by the fact that female teachers are positive role models for female students, thus creating a higher average score by improving the performance of girls. While female teachers are extremely important in most cultures of developing countries, the prevailing shortage of specialized teachers such as those of Science, Mathematics, and language (Bregman & Stallmeister, 2002; Warwick & Jatoi, 1994) is and remains to be serious obstacles on school outcomes. Most schools lack science teachers. Many schools are forced to use non-professional educators to teach Science, Mathematics, and languages.

Table 1.2.
Effect of Human Resource Variables on Student Achievement

Attribute	Effect	Magnitude of effect	Study
Parental involvement	+	Strong	Werf et al.,(2001),
Quality of principal			
Administrator experience	+	Strong	Lassibille & Tan (2001), Werf et al.,(2001), Willms & Somers (2001), Scheerens (2001b)
Administrator training	+	Not reported	Caillods et al., (1995)
Teacher quality			
Teacher training	+	Mixed (small & strong)	Anderson & Sumra (2002), Caillods et al., (1995), Kellaghan & Greaney (1992), Nyagura & Riddell (1993), Riddell & Nyagura (1991), Woessmann (2001),
	Nil		Lassibille & Tan (2001)
Teacher experience	+		Caillods et al.,(1995), Nyagura & Riddell (1993)
	-		Lassibille & Tan (2001), Wobmann (2000)
Teacher salaries	+	Not reported	Lopez-Acevedo & Salinas (2001), Wobmann (2002)
Teacher instruction time	+		Jimenez & Pinzon (1999), Velez et al.,(1993), Wobmann(2000)
Teacher turn-over	-		Riddell & Nyagura (1991)
Female teachers	+	Strong	Wobmann(2000), Nyagura & Riddell (1993), Warwick & Jatoi (1994),
Student-teachers ratio	-	Small	
Quality of students	+		Werf et al.,(2001), Willms & Somers (2001)
Students' socio-economic status	+	Strong	
Students' family background	+	Not reported	Wobmann (2003)

Apparently, many science teachers teach "out-of-field" (Ware, 1992a, p. v) in developing countries. Given that attracting and retaining qualified specialized teachers is a challenge and remains to be an important policy issue, considering the existing paucity of resources (Bregman & Stallmeister, 2002; Chapman & Mulkeen, 2003). Students attending schools without enough specialized teachers (of Science, Mathematics, and languages.) are clearly disadvantaged. Since Science, Mathematics, and languages are often compulsory subjects for all students attending secondary school, this lack of qualified teachers in those subjects seem to exert a negative influence on the final grade on examination results (J. M. Hite, Hite, Mugimu, Rew, & Nsubuga, 2004; K. M. Lewin & Gunne, 2000). It remains unclear which human resources in developing contexts are most robust in contributing to student performance. Whether schools with greater access to highly specialized teachers do better in terms of examination scores than other schools needs to be investigated.

WHERE IS THE GAP IN EE?

As indicated earlier, the great preponderance of EE studies have focused on the primary school level rather than the secondary school level (Figueredo & Anzolone, 2003; Fuller & Clarke, 1994; Scheerens, 2001b; Wyatt, 1996). The need therefore exists to investigate the impact of school resources on school performance at the secondary level.

Whether the impact of school resources on school performance is higher or lower at secondary level than at primary levels remains obscure (Fuller & Clarke, 1994). Whether the impact of resources on school performances vary between secondary schools in the developing countries and those of industrialized countries is not known. The following review focuses exclusively on issues at the secondary level of education.

RESOURCES AND SECONDARY EDUCATION IN DEVELOPING COUNTRIES

> Secondary education is indeed a crucial stage for the education system ... Students enter secondary schools as children and leave it as young adults. What they experience there will influence the course of the rest of their lives (Hernes, 2001, p. v).

The critical lack of school resources can undermine the quality of secondary education in developing countries (J. M. Hite, Mugimu, & Hite, 2002). Many secondary schools lack the basic infrastructure, facilities, and resources that are important for student learning. Therefore, the majority of disadvantaged youth in developing countries are not likely to receive quality secondary education (Bregman & Stallmeister, 2001; Bregman & Stallmeister, 2002; K. M. Lewin, 2001a, 2001c; WorldBank, 2003). Yet, secondary education can and should contribute in a fundamental way to the knowledge and skills needed for individuals to become productive citizens and to be competitive on the global job market (Alvarez & Bradsher, 2003; Hernes, 2001). Since educational knowledge is the "most powerful engine of production...[and therefore,] the most important component of human capital" (Schultz, 1993, p. 16-17). Given this fundamental role of education to human capital development, most governments have focused their efforts on providing universal primary education (UPE) in the post-Jomtien era while neglecting secondary education (Serrant & McClure, 2003; UNESCO, 1994). Granted that primary education offers much higher social rates of return than secondary education. However, given the bulging numbers of UPE graduates who increasingly demand opportunities for secondary education, there is need to expand secondary education (UNESCO, 1997, 2001). Failure to do so would undermine the efforts of expanding and improving the quality of universal primary education.

Indeed, while secondary education is critical, it remains a neglected level of education by many governments in developing countries (Figueredo & Anzolone, 2003). This neglect of secondary education is consistent with the contemporary notion that girls' and basic education provides higher social rates of return than secondary and tertiary education in developing nations (Psacharopoulos, 1994). Consequently, available empirical studies at the secondary level are extremely few, let alone studies that deal with the role of school resources and school outcomes in developing countries (Fuller, et al., 1993).

This is a condition that is more interesting when considering that secondary education typically costs more than primary education (Fuller, et al., 1993; Garfield, Holsinger, & Ziderman, 1994; K. M. Lewin & Caillods, 2001). Figueredo and Anzolone (2003) indicated "in the least developed countries, each secondary school student costs on average about 3.5 times more than primary school student" (p. 11). It becomes extremely difficult, therefore, to mobilize and gain access to basic school resources and vital material needed for providing quality secondary education in the context of resource scarcity (UNESCO, 2001; Yeom & McClure, 2001). According to Figueredo and Anzolone (2003), many secondary schools in developing countries do not meet the minimum quality standards.

To a significant degree, this lack of focus on the secondary education component of developing country systems can be attributed to the rightly vigorous emphasis placed on UPE in the post-Jomtien era (ADEA, 2003; UNESCO, 1994, 2003a). While the world has taken great strides toward universalizing access to primary education, the next necessary step is to investigate the improvement of the secondary system. Indeed, without knowledge of how to improve secondary education in the developing countries of the world, where will all of the primary school graduates, produced by the tremendous global post-Jomtien efforts, go for more education?

CONCLUSION

Very little is known about the critical resources that actually contribute to school performance in secondary education. Whether secondary schools having greater access to specific critical resources are likely to outperform other schools which lack such resources remains a vitally important, under-researched policy question. The past decade has seen a booming expansion of the private sector to supplement public provision of secondary education in many developing countries (Bennell & Sayed, 2002b; Bradshaw, 1993; J. M. Hite, et al., 2002; Tooley, 2001). Furthermore, the expanding private sector for secondary schools increases the competition for procuring critical scarce resources. Schools that are capable of strategically competing for and using available but scarce resources on vital education programs (Gyimah-Brempong, 2003) and capable of reducing costs (Thulstrup, 1999) are more likely to perform and persist better than other schools. A fruitful strategic perspective for framing the educational effort to increase the availability of quality secondary schooling, while being competitive in that effort, is the Resource-Based View (RBV) (Barney, 2002). The RBV as described below provides a framework for examining the influence of specific resources on school performance. This is addressed in detail in Chapter two.

CHAPTER TWO

RESOURCE-BASED VIEW: LOCAL PESPECTIVES

Building upon the seminal work of Edith Penrose in her book entitled 'The Theory of the Growth of the Firm', researchers have developed the strategic RBV of organizational performance (Foss, 2000, 2002; Penrose, 1959, 1995; Rugman & Verbeke, 2002). Penrose (1959) observed that an organization consists of a bundle of resources that are heterogeneous. In her view, these heterogeneous resources can potentially yield services that can be delivered by an organization. Organizations are heterogeneous in the sense that different organizations have different kinds of resources (Penrose, 1959), which they use to sustain their superior performance (Barney, 1991a). Building on Penrose's ideas, many researchers developed and established the RBV as a valuable perspective on explaining organization performance based on organization's resources (Barney, 1986, 1989, 1991b, 1996; Barney & Zajac, 1994; Conner, 1991; Conner & Prahalad, 1996; Peteraf, 1993; Rouse & Daellenbach, 1999; Rumelt, 1984, 1991). The RBV has identified many types of resources such as financial, physical and human resources (Barney, 2002; J. M. Hite, et al., 2002; Marsh & Ranft, 1999). Financial resources include school fees, capitation grant, capital development funds, donations, and loans. Physical resources include school building facilities, classrooms, staff housing, vehicles, instructional materials, farm tools, office and science equipment, school's geographical location, athletics facilities, and so on. Human resources include teachers' qualifications, teachers' experience, gender, prior students' achievement, students' socio-economic status, and so on.

In recent years, RBV seems to "influence theoretical and empirical studies done in non-strategic management disciplines such as human resource management, marketing, management information systems and operation research" (Barney & Arikan, 2001, p. 124). Increasingly RBV is also beginning to be used in education-related research (Amis, Pant, & Slack, 1997; Luxton, Farrelly, & Salmon, 2000; Nixon, Bishop, Clouse, & Kemelgor, 2003). Furthermore, the growing body of RBV research has generated numerous attributes or conditions that resources must have in order to enable the organizations to gain superior performance (Barney, 1986; Jugdev & Thomas, 2002; Wernerfelt, 1984).

Barney (1991a) postulated that for a resource to be advantage creating (in terms of organization performance) in a sustainable manner, it must be: valuable, rare, inimitable, and non-substitutable. In addition, the advantage-creating resource must also be exploitable by the organization to realize sustainable superior performance (Barney, 2002; Barney & Wright, 1998).

Based on Barney's five resource attributes, this dissertation utilized the VRISE framework (V = Valuable, R = Rare, I = Inimitable, S = Non-Substitutable, and E = Exploitable by Organization), which was adapted from Barney (2002). Table 2.1 shows that a school having resources that do not possess any of the Barney's five resource attributes is unlikely to realize even temporary superior performance. Conversely, a school having resources that possess all Barney's five resource attributes is very likely to enjoy sustainable superior performance beyond other schools. Any resource that demonstrates three or four of Barney's attributes could be considered a "critical" resource in that these would possess sufficient competitive value that having them would be critical to establishing and maintaining a competitive advantage in the school marketplace. Further discussion of the VRISE framework is covered in later chapters.

Table 2.1.
Relationships Between VRISE Framework and Superior Performance

Is a resource...

Valuable?	Rare?	Inimitable?	Non-Substitutable?	Exploitable by Organization?	Superior Performance
No				Most Unlikely	Most Unlikely
Yes	No			Less Likely	Less Likely
Yes	Yes	No		Somewhat Likely	Somewhat Likely
Yes	Yes	Yes	No	Likely	Likely
Yes	Yes	Yes	Yes	Most Likely	Most Likely

Adapted from Barney (2002, p. 173-174)

> Resources and capabilities can be heterogeneously distributed across competing firms [organizations], that these differences can be long lasting, and can help explain why some firms consistently outperform others. From this perspective, the RBV actually consists of a rich body of related, yet distinct theoretical tools with which to analyze firm level sources of sustained competitive advantage (Barney, 2001b, p. 649).

Educational organizations must offer, and deliver, much more by making available quality educational opportunities to meet the needs of an increasingly dynamic and changing society. This public expectation of educational organizations must be accomplished amidst an acknowledged and critical paucity of educational resources. Recognizing that schools broadly and consistently differ in quality, particularly in developing countries, stakeholders and educational planners are confronted with this one key policy challenge: How to strategically improve the quality of educational services in all schools in a context of increasingly scarce educational resources. Without stakeholders actually knowing which of those current resources are most productive and best contribute to student performance, their ability to make informed decisions is severely limited (Chapman & Mahlck, 1993; J. M. Hite, Hite, Rew, Mugimu, & Nsubuga, 2004; Mugimu & Hite, 2001).

A need exists to link specific resources with student and school performance in educational organizations. Past efforts have relied, with mixed results at best, on simple production-function models (Picus, 1997; Richards, 1991b).

However, the strategic perspective of RBV provides "fresh" theoretical tools that could help explain the relationships between advantage-creating resources and superior performance in educational organizations in ways previously not possible.

EMERGING THEORY

The RBV offers a great promise to understand resources and performance better in educational organizations. In her seminal work The Theory of the Growth of the Firm, Edith Penrose (1959) introduced imaginative ideas about the resources and performance of organizations that has led to expanding use of the RBV by a number of influential organizational theorists (Barney, 1986, 1989, 1991a; Conner, 1991; Foss, 2002; Penrose, 1959, 1995; Rouse & Daellenbach, 1999; Rugman & Verbeke, 2002; Rumelt, 1984; Wernerfelt, 1984). Penrose (1959) postulated that an organization consists of a bundle of productive resources that are heterogeneous. In her view, heterogeneous resources can potentially yield services that can be offered by an organization. Organizations are heterogeneous in the sense that different organizations have different kinds of resources (Penrose, 1959) that they use to maintain their competitively superior performance (Barney, 2002).

Other subsequent researchers have endorsed the importance of the heterogeneous resources that organizations use to implement strategies that can lead to superior organizational performance (Barney, 1986, 1991a; Grant, 1991; Wernerfelt, 1984). This perspective proposes that "there are systematic differences across organizations in the extent to which they control resources that are necessary for implementing strategies, and that these differences are relatively stable" (Foss, 2000, p. 14). Educational organizations are therefore different because they have different resources and capabilities and also differ in how they use these resources. Simply recognizing that educational organizations are different because they have different resources explains, to a great extent, why certain educational organizations consistently outperform others, while other schools may consistently lag behind the rest in terms of performance.

KEY ASSUMPTIONS OF THE RESOURCE-BASED VIEW

The RBV is based on two basic assumptions including: (1) resource heterogeneity and (2) resource immobility (Barney, 1991a; Barney & Arikan, 2001; Peteraf, 1993). According to Barney & Arikan (2001), resource heterogeneity is the idea that competing organizations may control different bundles of productive resources. Resource immobility denotes the notion that these differences in organizational resources may be consistently lasting (Barney & Arikan, 2001) or that the organization is not at risk of loosing them. However, simply because an organization possesses resources that are both heterogeneous and immobile may not guarantee that those resources will be translated into good use and profitable strategies (Peteraf, 1993). Is it not self-defeating for a school to make available an adequate stock of library textbooks without actually making necessary provisions for students to use the textbooks? How then, can students gain knowledge and improve on their performance without actually having the opportunity to use library resources (i.e. textbooks)?

While possessing different superior resources (such as computers) is vital for an educational organization, simply possessing those resources may not be sufficient. This is due to the fact that resources are only useful if they are used to generate marketable services such as good examination scores, students graduating with competitive job skills, and so on. Thus, contemporary educational managers are confronted with the challenge of properly planning how to use critical educational resources efficiently and effectively. An educational organization (school) may be efficient but not effective, or effective but not efficient, in putting critical resources to good use (Levacic & Glover, 1997). In recent years, there has been increasing demand for accountability, efficiency, and equity in resource utilization and optimization in education that can be demonstrated through the numerous hot policy debates on these important issues (Cooper, Fusarelli, & Randall, 2004; Tsang, 2002). Stakeholders are demanding that schools provide the best value for their money in terms of improved examination scores and educational quality.

Educational organizations must prove their worth by showing their ability to "conceive of, implement, and exploit valuable resources" (Mata, Fuerst, & Barney, 1995, p. 491) and also to ensure that students have the ability to use these resources, which is extremely important if educational organizations are to excel in performance. Furthermore, "some organizations may possess resources that enable them to develop more effectively and implement additional profitable strategies than other [organizations]" (Barney & Arikan, 2001). Thus, trying to understand why it is so in educational organizations remains a critical policy issue. Even though "heterogeneity is the most basic condition necessary for sustainable advantage...it is not sufficient" (Peteraf, 1993 p, 185). Educational organizations need to realize that critical resources must be identified; developed, and maintained in order to generate useful marketable services. Therefore, educational managers must realize how vital and necessary it is to identify the critical productive resources of their institutions.

For educational managers, being able to isolate, nurture, and maintain critical productive resources of an educational organization is crucial. However, while this notion of identifying critical resources in educational organizations may sound easy and straightforward, unfortunately it is very difficult for most stakeholders in educational organizations. Collis and Montgomery (1995) explained that "because managers tend to take their organizational resources as given, they have hard time in identifying and evaluating their organization's resources objectively" (p.120). Additionally, a school principal may find it extremely difficult to know who the key players are in contributing to his/her school's success: for instance parents, students, teachers, community, politicians, or the church minister of his faith.

While identifying and evaluating future educational organization resources is vital, focusing on the already available critical resources can provide added advantage for leveraging resource value. Barney (1986) indicates that an organization may gain exceptional advantages if it analyzes the resources it already has. Furthermore, organizations are likely to excel if they can optimize the use of their own specialized resources (Peteraf, 1993). In economic terms, it becomes cheaper in the long run to exploit current resources rather than seek out new resources. Nonetheless, a potential problem may arise if an educational organization is stuck with their current resources without actually attempting to tap into alternative provisions that could boost improved efficiency and effectiveness of the institution. Teece, Pisano, & Shuen (1990) contend that resources endowments are "sticky," that is, "firms are stuck with what they have and must live with what they lack" [italics added] (p. 8). Consequently, as Koruna and Luggen (2003) pointed out, "Many great ideas within firms go unnoticed as they do not get to the top management's support" (p. 21), thus firms get stuck in the daily routines and strictly exploiting current resources.

Notwithstanding that to focus only on current resources may tend to discourage innovation, creativity, and flexibility, which are currently crucial if schools are to meet the ever-changing educational demands of the global society. For instance, a school may have staff members with long teaching experience—who may be reluctant to adapt to necessary curriculum reforms or to new advancing technology (Hargreaves & Fullan, 1998) because they do not want to let go of their old teaching practices. This tendency may of course undermine the school's efforts towards exploring and taking advantage of cutting edge technology etc.

Given the dynamic, changing society, educational organizations must be able to and should focus on "value-creating resources that are difficult to imitate" (Peteraf, 1993) with reasonable flexibility. This strategy can be fundamentally critical for many educational organizations. However, exploiting difficult to imitate resources may not be as easy as it sounds for every institution because not all resources are equally productive for all educational organizations. Since what works well for one school may not do so for another. The paradox remains that different educational organizations can generate different kinds of marketable services from comparably similar resources. For instance, in Uganda, it is not uncommon for a teacher to be shared by two different schools and produce totally different results in each school. Thus, no clear-cut answers seem to explain issues related to resource heterogeneity and performance in educational organizations.

The quest to understand the relationship between resources and performance in organizations has guided and motivated RBV theorists such as Penrose, Wernerfelt, Barney, and others. Increasingly, effective educational researchers may utilize RBV in their attempt to understand better the relationship between resources and performance in educational organizations. An important resource issue is that, based on empirical research, specific resource attributes are and can be associated with superior performance of organizations.

RESOURCE ATTRIBUTES: SUPERIOR ORGANIZATION PERFORMANCE

Not all resources are equally productive as value-creating resources. Resources have different qualities or attributes that enable them to become value-creating resources. Understanding the attributes of an organization's resource endowments may thus reveal more about organization performance (Wernerfelt, 1995). The RBV empirical work has generated extensive knowledge about numerous organizational resource attributes or conditions necessary to enable organizations to gain superior performance (Barney, 1986, 1991a; Collis & Montgomery, 1995; Foss, 2000; Jugdev & Thomas, 2002; Peteraf, 1993; Wernerfelt, 1984). For example, Barney (1991) introduced four attributes that advantage-creating resources must have: value, rarity, inimitability, and non-substitutability.

As earlier indicated this research draws on the Resource-Based View perspective especially focusing on the VRISE framework, which comprised five resource attributes first suggested by Barney (1991) and then expanded upon by other numerous RBV theorists (Amit & Schoemaker, 1993; Collis & Montgomery, 1995; Grant, 1991). Two reasons exist for adapting the VRISE (V = valuable, R = Rare, I = Inimitable, S = Non-Substitutable, and E = Exploitable by the organization) framework. First, these five attributes are consistent with the key assumptions of RBV (i.e. resource heterogeneity and resource immobility). Second, the framework entailed in applying these attributes provides a valuable interpretive and explanatory framework not available in previous production-function applications in EE research.

Lack of an adequately sensitive and powerful explanatory framework has generated serious debate as to the utility of EE research in general, and in production-function applications specifically. Each of these attributes is briefly presented and discussed in the following sections.

Value

According to Fahy & Smithee (1999) the potential of a resource to contribute superior organization performance lies in its importance to facilitate value-creation. To create value, a resource will sustain a product or service that customers are willing to pay for (Collis & Montgomery, 1995). Who would want to invest in a resource that has no value? Fahy and Smithee (1999) contended that value to customers is an essential element of superior organization performance. Value-creation is also extremely vital in performance of educational organizations. No parent would like to enroll his/her child in a failing school, whose students never learn anything. Parents and the public not only want to see results, but the results must be good. This explains why better performing schools have higher student enrollment and therefore lower unit costs than struggling schools. However, knowledge gaps exist in research examining which organizational resources offer the most value to customers (Fahy & Smithee, 1999), particularly in educational organizations.

Given that valuable resources may be tangible, less tangible, or intangible (Collis & Montgomery, 1995), their examination becomes rather complicated and problematic. Several scholars have indicated the complexity of evaluating resources because value is determined by the interplay with potentially complex market forces (Collis & Montgomery, 1995). For example, what is shown to be a critically valuable resource in a grocery store may fail to have any value in a school due to different market forces. Alignment of value creation with the needed services therefore becomes an important challenge confronting educational organizations. Vignette 2.1 presents an example of school resources that create value.

Vignette 2.1. School Bus/Truck

In a developing context, there are extremely few schools that can own school buses or trucks. Owning a school bus or truck adds great value to the school and hence competitive advantage. The school bus or truck can be used for transportation of students, teachers, building materials, foods, and other school materials, thus cutting down transportation costs relative to the cost of hiring vehicles from public means.

Additionally, other schools can hire the school bus or truck, thus generating extra revenue for the school. These additional funds allow the school to implement a wider range of educational programs that could lead to improved school performance.

The school bus or truck not only enables the school to reduce transportation costs, but also it is one way to advertise and market the school. Many parents and students could be attracted to schools owning their own transportation.

Thus, successful schools need to identify which resources are valuable that could give them a competitive "edge". Schools must also, however, identify which resources are rare. Resources must not only be valuable, but also be rare to enable the organization to maximize and improve its efficiency and effectiveness (Barney, 1991a; Fahy, 2000).

Rareness

A resource is rare if extremely few educational organizations have access to it. According to the RBV, if a few organizations control a value-creating resource or strategy that is uncommon or rare, then these organizations will enjoy a competitive advantage provided they conceive of and implement strategies pertaining to superior performance (Barney, 1991a; Koruna & Luggen, 2003). However, rarity of an organization's resources does not guarantee superiority in performance. Controlling a rare resource is not enough; it must be put into good use in order for the educational organization to gain superior performance. Securing a value-creating rare resource is one thing; being able to utilize that value-creating, rare resource to implement strategies that lead to superior performance may be another. Vignette 2.1 illustrates how a rare and potentially valuable resource was obtained, but not properly utilized to competitive advantage in one school in Uganda.

Inimitability

In the example in vignette 2.2, being connected to electricity is costly within a developing context. While schools may find substitutes in generators or solar energy both of these substitutes may also be substantially costly. Inimitable resources are usually costly or difficult to copy, thus, "inimitability is the heart of value creation"(Collis & Montgomery, 1995, p. 120). Competitor schools may have hard time strategically creating equivalent substitutes for resources that are inimitable, which thus hinders them from producing similar services on the open market. Thus, a school that controls inimitable resource enjoys greater competitive advantage. Vignette 2.3 illustrates the advantages of having inimitable resources.

Therefore, even when a school invests in more organizational resources than other schools, they may not necessarily enjoy superior performance unless those resources are inimitable (Barney, 1991a; Fahy, 2000). A school controlling a resource that is easy to copy, duplicate, or substitute generates only temporary value to the organization (Hitt, Ireland, & Hoskisson, 2001). Nevertheless, "inimitability does not last forever. Competitors eventually find ways to copy the most valuable resources" (Collis & Montgomery, 1995, p. 121). This is particularly true given the rapid advancements in technology and the global economic forces that now cross cultural boundaries.

Vignette 2.2. **School A and Computers Donated from the U.S.**

In 1993, High School A received a donation of five computers from the United States worth US$ 5,000. The computers were delivered to the school, and the school principal kept them in one corner of his hot-dusty small office. None of the faculty members in High School A had even a slight knowledge of how to use computers. Indeed, none of them actually knew what to do with the computers at all. Furthermore, the main electric power supply to the school was too low to run the computers, given that the school's electricity was 220 volts and the computers were designed to run on 110 volts. Utilizing this one resource would require purchasing several expensive electric converters, i.e. from 220V to 110V – which would thus consume even more precious resources. In addition, the electric power supply was extremely inconsistent creating a need for the purchase of an electric generator (yet another drain on scarce resources).

With the limited financial resources, High School A's administration could not make the necessary provisions to purchase of the generator, converters, and set up a computer room (an air-conditioned and dust-free room). Five years later, the new computers had turned into breeding homes for rats and cockroaches. Eventually, these computers were removed from the principal's office and were moved to the store. The once-promising rare resource of computers rusted and became unusable. High School A never benefited in any substantial school program from gaining access to these computers, even though they were a rare resource.

Vignette 2.3. Namasagali College

Namasagali College is a private secondary school founded on a Catholic foundation located in Kamuli District, Uganda. This college is popularly known for its excellence in extra-curricula activities or programs (music, dance, and drama).

For over twenty years, each year, Namasagali College usually leads in the national drama and music competitions held at the National Theatre. Over the years, this college has specialized and developed students' abilities in drama and music to the extent that none of the other schools can beat them.

Numerous parents and students are attracted by the unique and rich curriculum in extra-curricular programs offered by the school. By simply concentrating on these programs and doing them well, Namasagali College, has built its own reputation that is extremely difficult for other schools to match, copy or duplicate.

Many students who are well-recognized men and women in the arts, both locally and internationally, have gone through Namasagali College. The graduates of this college are excellent ambassadors and agents for the school and have marketed the school. While it is difficult to believe, Namasagali College does not have enough places for all the students that apply each year.

Non-Substitutability

Non-substitutable resources denote that there are few or no alternative resources that can produce the same services. "A resource is non-substitutable when no other resources can enable the organization to conceive of and implement the same strategies as efficiently and effectively as the original resource" (Barney & Arikan, 2001, p. 141). Organizations with imperfectly substitutable resources enjoy competitive advantage (Barney, 1991a).

An organization's position on the market can be seriously threatened if competing organizations offer, or begin to offer, similar services or products to customers at lower prices or in a more effective fashion (Collis & Montgomery, 1995). This is why private schooling raising the bar for public schools due to increased competition among schools has become one of the hot debates (Cooper, et al., 2004; Tsang, 2002). If an educational organization relies upon substitutable resources, the performance of that organization may be destabilized. For example, another school may also secure examiners and therefore improve and excels in the national public examinations. As a result, the competing school will be able to win the goodwill of parents and students. An example of non-substitutable resources is found among the religious schools (Catholic, Moslems, and Protestant founded schools). These schools have an assured clientele because they have a valued resource that is non-substitutable – religious perspective. However, if a non-religious school is taken over by a particular dominant religious group, then it may also be able to tap into and compete for that same clientele. Vignette 2.4 provides another illustration of non-substitutable resources.

> *Vignettee 2.4.* Piped Running Water and Flush Toilets
>
> Very few schools in Uganda have piped running water and flush toilets. Installing piped running water and a flush toilet system is extremely costly to duplicate and thus the majority of schools cannot afford it. Once a school has piped running water and flush toilets systems set up, these systems are valuable, rare, and non-transferable. Yet, these facilities can neither be moved and nor shared by other schools.
>
> A school possessing piped running water and flush toilets enjoys a greater competitive advantage than others. Since access to clean water and toilets improves sanitary conditions and creates a better learning environment, richer parents are attracted to enroll their students in schools with these resources. Additionally, parents are generally more willing to pay for better educational services; hence, the school will have greater access to more financial resources than others. Additional financial resources could facilitate the implementation of extra educational programs, which may boost school performance and competitive advantage.

Exploitable by the Organization

Possession of a value-creating resource that cannot be exploited by the organization does not lead to superior performance. While such resources are typically vital, they are not sufficiently powerful in a competitive sense without also being functional or useable by the organization (Peteraf & Bergen, 2003). An example of this condition would be High School A presented in Vignette 2.4. Particularly, the resource of the financially valuable and typically rare computers received from the United States. Although these computers were both valuable and rare, School A was unable to exploit them to gain superior performance. Given that High School A lacked the capacity to exploit the computers.

RBV EMPIRICAL STUDIES

The RBV has been used in empirical research to assess the impact of various resources on the performance and competitiveness of organizations. Most studies have looked at resources and performance in fields of industrial management, organization behavior, human resource management, and strategic management (Barney, 2001a; Bourke, 2000; Hitt, Bierman, Shimizu, & Kochhar, 2001; Maijoor & Witteloostuijn, 1996; Miller & Shamse, 1996). Numerous empirical studies have attempted to examine the influence of resource endowments on organizational performance (Durand, 1999; Wernerfelt & Montgomery, 1988). Appendix A shows some examples of RBV empirical studies. In these studies, scholars sought to "understand the complex interplay between different resources which lead to increases in performance" (Durand, 1999, p. 68). McEvily (1999) reported that one way of testing the Resource-Based View is to identify which resources account for the superior performance of an organization. Nevertheless, RBV theorists are beginning to extend their work into educational organizations. The following section will briefly discuss empirical RBV studies in the field of education.

RBV STUDIES IN EDUCATIONAL ORGANIZATIONS

Increasingly, RBV is being applied in fields related to educational research and planning. Considering the declining resources and increasing competition in education, strategic positioning of educational institutions has never been so important. Luxton, Farrelly & Salmon (2000) examined whether two attributes, "on-line educational value" and "barriers to duplication" created quality advantage in resources in the establishment and maintenance of the eMaster of Marketing program in distance education. Luxton et al., (2000) conceptualized resources based on what represents on-line educational value, and what provides the barriers to duplication of the on-line educational value in the context of the eMaster of Marketing program. They concluded that adopting the RBV offered knowledge and skills to facilitate effective transfer of critical development and delivery capabilities to promote continuous quality advantage in the key resources in the eMaster of Marketing education program. Luxton et al., (2000) indicated that by simply identifying barriers to duplication resource attributes of the distance education program, they were able to create and improve the quality of presentations and delivery standards of their learning modules. While maintaining consistency across all subjects in a unique manner that added value, the eMaster of Marketing quality enabled the program to enjoy a competitive advantage on the global market.

Nixon, Bishop, Clouse and Kemelgor (2003) also used variables including value, rarity, imperfect inimitability, and entrepreneurial fitness to examine how entrepreneurs could develop new wealth-generating opportunities in an educational setting. Nixon et al.'s (2003) study revealed that a systematic search for entrepreneurial discoveries can be taught and applied in educational settings to yield results. While RBV research in educational settings is not extensive, it has potential for schools that are driven by marketplace forces.

APPLYING RBV AT THE SCHOOL LEVEL

Schools compete for financial, human and physical resources. Therefore competition is not alien to schools. Empirical evidence indicates that schools with highly skilled teachers show higher performance (Willms & Somers, 2001). Furthermore, those schools that enroll gifted students also perform better (Rutter, 1983). Selective schools tend to engage more trained teachers and better students, hence higher performance in national examinations. As a result parents and student tend to be attracted to these schools (Fuller & Clarke, 1994). Indeed, numerous resources are highlighted as being related to school outcomes, but those that best contribute to school performance and why they do so, are not clearly spelled out.

When it comes to determining what resources create the most advantages for educational organizations and how to access them, the decision is still somewhat speculative. For instance, it has been suggested that resource sharing can boost new schools as they develop relationships with older schools, for instance through administrators and teachers. Thus the network is developed as a school resource (Hill & Guthrie, 1999; J. M. Hite, et al., 2002). Many advantages exist for meaningful network systems that can promote struggling schools and their students toward accessing better resources and achieving greater success in their educational programs (Adekanmbi, Kamou, & Mphinyane, 1996; J. M. Hite, et al., 2002). The argument is also raised that when school principals network (coordinating with others), they tend to leverage their resources and capabilities. Hargreaves (2002) suggested that the idea of leveraging strategies for educational inputs and outputs in a school as a possibility to improve school quality, especially in situations where resources are scarce. Furthermore, the notion of developing social capital—establishing trust, mutual reliance, and reciprocity among stakeholders of an organization— is another potentially positive approach (Hill & Guthrie, 1999; Tamukong, 1997). However, no empirical evidence is yet available to show whether secondary school principals who take advantage of networks as resources, influence their school's performance, and outperform other schools. This is one example of how the relationship between school resources and school performance needs further research.

CONCLUSION

When researchers work outside their box in terms of paradigm shift, they may gain a new ontological view in interpreting data on school resources and performance. RBV can be a valuable tool to the researchers of school resources and school performance, by bringing a wide range of different perspectives. Thus, allowing objectivity and subjectivity for them to make appropriate inferences while recognizing the diverse cultural contexts especially in the developing countries. In view of the fact that private schooling and private schools are increasingly becoming the major providers of educational services, many private schools today are operating as for-profit business organizations, so they need to be managed efficiently in order to maximize the profits by attempting to offer educational services that are value for the money spent.

Recognizing that majority of these schools are under-resourced, this tends to compromise the quality of education. The ability of educators to identify, nurture, value creating resources may lead to better schooling conditions for the children. Schools may be in a better position to maximize their profits, realize greater success and become more effective. Chapter three discusses the status of secondary education and highlights its pivotal role in the lives of the world's children.

CHAPTER THREE

STATUS OF SECONDARY EDUCATION IN UGANDA

Secondary schools receive primary pupils, train them and eventually send them to tertiary institutions, thus occupy a central position in the education system. The Ugandan education system (see Figure 3.1) consists of two years of pre-primary school, seven years of primary school, four years of lower secondary school, two years of upper secondary school, and two to six years of post-secondary education.

Recent years have seen great emphasis on efforts to provide basic education for all, through the implementation of Universal Primary Education (UPE) (Holsinger, Mugimu, & Jacob, 2001; Tomasevski, 1999). These trends and developments in expanding UPE have influenced the demand for secondary education. Further elaboration of UPE policy and its impact on the Secondary Education is imperative.

THE IMPACT OF UPE POLICY ON SECONDARY EDUCATION IN UGANDA

UNESCO's 1990 worldwide education conference held in Jomtien, Thailand, was the focal point in helping developing countries toward refocusing their attention to basic education. The renewed emphasis on basic education was demonstrated when nearly all participating countries committed themselves to providing every child, youth, and adult with educational opportunities to meet their basic learning needs (UNESCO, 1994). The target set at the Jomtien Conference for all signatory nations was to achieve Universal Primary Education (UPE) by the year 2000.

Like most signatories, the Ugandan government recognized that bridging the basic education gap would be one of the most important strategies to eradicate poverty, to promote social development, and to foster economic growth. The government commitment for UPE was demonstrated in the new 1995 constitution, which states, "all persons have a right to education." This constitutional declaration obligated the state to provide basic education to all its citizens through UPE (Tomasevski, 1999). In 1996, the implementation of UPE policy began, and the Ugandan government targeted complete achievement of UPE by 2003.

In 1997 alone, the year when the UPE policy was inaugurated, student enrollment in all UPE schools shot up from 3.4 million to over 5.4 million, and then to over 7.0 million by 2002 (Murphy, 2003). Figure 3.2 shows that overall student enrollments are higher in lower division classes than higher. Pupil enrollment peaked in 1997, the year when the government committed to providing free education to four children per family. In subsequent years, pupil enrollment rates remained consistently high. Figure was adopted from MOES (2002).

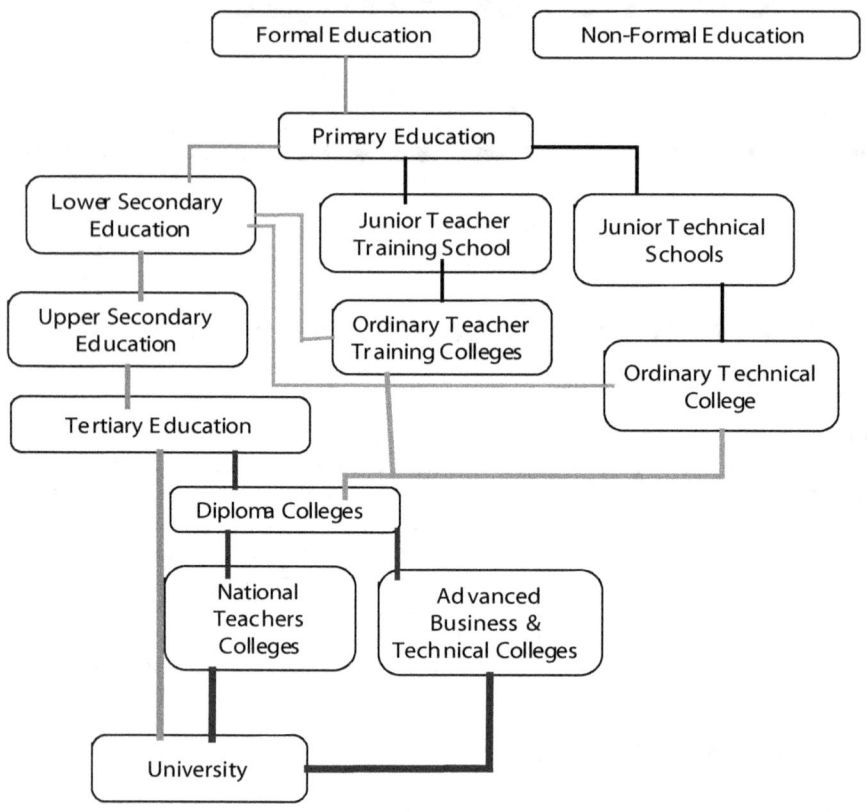

Figure 3.1 . Structure of Ugandan Education System

The exploding numbers of pupils in primary education created a potentially overwhelming demand for places in secondary education. A similar situation is reported in many other developing countries such as Tanzania (Lassibille, Tan, & Sumra, 2000; Mutakyahwa, 1999), South Korea (Kim, 2001), and Zimbabwe (Machingaidze, et al., 1998). Throughout this era there were not enough places at the secondary level of education to accommodate all the UPE graduates completing the primary cycle. The Ugandan government did not have enough resources to create and support enough secondary schools, let alone primary schools (WorldBank, 2002).

Figure 3.3 shows the primary and secondary students enrollment from 1996 to 2001 (data was obtained from MOES, 2002). Clearly, comparing numbers of primary pupils' enrollment are astronomical relative to secondary students' enrollment. As a result of increasing students' enrollment at both primary and secondary levels, the past seven years have seen an enormous growth of the secondary sector, particularly through private provision.

Chapter 3 - Status of Secondary Education in Uganda

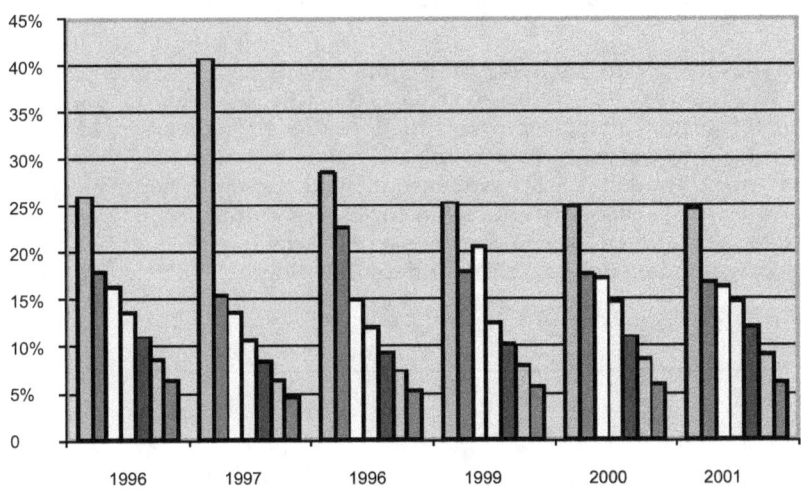

Figure 3.2. Percentage Enrollment Distributions by Class 1996-2001

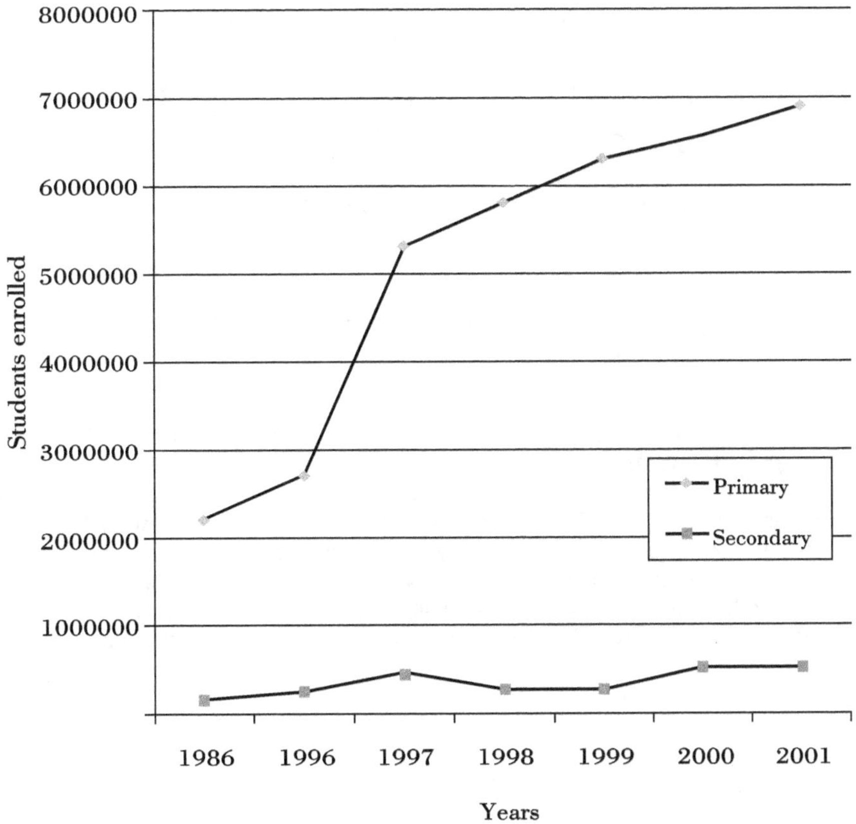

Figure 3.3. Primary and Secondary Enrollments 1986-2001.

Figure 3.4 shows secondary school growth from 1996 to 2001 based on Planning Unit data from the Ministry of Education and Sports (MOES, 2004). Figure 3.4 reveals the rapid growth of secondary sector from 621 in 1998 to 2,400 secondary schools in 2001. That is, almost four times increase in the secondary sector in only three years. However, Chapman and Mahlck (1993) have contended that uncontrolled rapid growth of private and government secondary education could be counterproductive in terms of declining quality of education. Given that most schools lack basic facilities needed for rudimentary educational environments (Anderson & Sumra, 2002; Liang, 2002).

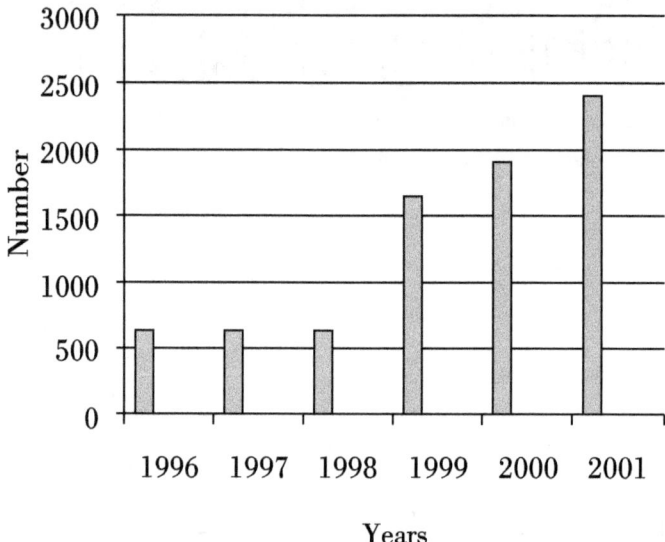

Figure 3.4. Secondary School Growths 1996-2001

For example, Figure 3.5 indicates shortage (in percentages) of basic physical resources in secondary schools in Uganda based on School Census 2000 data. This shortage of basic resources in facilities within the fast-growing context of both primary and secondary sectors is a big concern to policy makers in education. Indeed, World Bank (2001) cautioned countries that "growing enrollments must not obscure the fact that quality of education provided is crucial" (p. 8), especially when different private and government providers of education exist.

The following section discusses private and government aided secondary schools in relation to resources, access, and educational quality.

Chapter 3 - Status of Secondary Education in Uganda

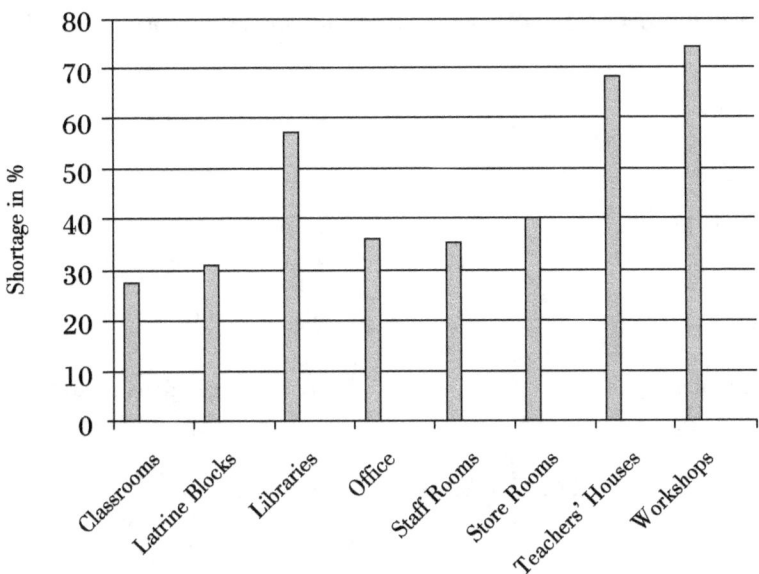

Figure 3.5. Shortages (%) of Basic Physical Resources at Secondary Schools3

PRIVATE VERSUS GOVERNMENT-AIDED SECONDARY SCHOOLS

In the colonial and post - colonial era, governments of many developing countries have provided major financing and subsidies for secondary education (Fuller, et al., 1993). However, Lewin (2001b) reports that this trend has changed in recent years.

Considering that most developing countries are faced with dwindling resources and over-burdened national budgets, they cannot cope with the increasing demand for places in secondary education (Fuller, et al., 1993; Lassibille, et al., 2000; K. M. Lewin, 2001b; Tilak, 1992). Coupled with decreasing public expenditures for education in many developing countries (Harber & Davies, 1997), an ever-expanding need exists to create alternative ways of providing for secondary education particularly.

Important characteristics of government-aided versus private schools in Uganda are presented in Table 3.1. As can be seen, numerous substantial differences exist between these two types of schools. The elements of governance and accountability are likely to present the most significant discrepancy between these schools that could lead to differences in quality of teaching and learning (Bregman & Stallmeister, 2002).

Table 3.1:

Characteristics of Government - Aided and Private Secondary Schools in Uganda

Government-Aided	Private
Founding Body	
- Religious groups Catholic, Anglican, Muslims	- Individuals - Communities - Non-governmental organizations (NGOs) - Religious groups
Ownership	
- Government/municipalities	- Individuals, religious groups, or NGOs
Governance	
- Greater state control through Board of Governors (BOG) and local governments - Less autonomous	- Self control and minimal government invdvement - More autonomous
Accountability	
- School managers are answerable to Ministry of Education and Sports (MoES) - Local political leader so influential	- More answerable to clients and public - Local political leaders less influential
Government-aided	Private
Resource Management	
- Books of accounts are mandatory	- Usually self-accounting
Financing/Resourcing	
- Receives direct support from government in form of teachers' salaries, laboratory equipment, textbooks, and capitation grants - Charge school fees for tuition from parents and students - BOG and Parent-Teacher Association (PTA) play major roles in soliciting additional funds - Receives donation and grants from international agencies through the MOES	- Do not receive direct support from government - Self-financing - Employ their own teachers; mobilize their own additional funds from friends, commercial banks, fundraising activities, etc. - Charge school fees for tuition from parents and student - BOG and PTA less functional

Chapter 3 - Status of Secondary Education in Uganda

Rapid Expansion of Private Sector and Resources

Interestingly, most developing countries have witnessed a rapid growth of private sector input to relieve the pressure on the overburdened systems and to expand access to secondary education (Tilak, 1992; Tooley, 2002). For example, Liang (2002) reported that private secondary schools in Uganda accounted for over 57 percent of the student enrollment in 2000.

Lewin (2002) also reported similar findings. Majority of students now attending private secondary schools in Uganda come from the poorest families, except in the very few elite private schools that target the rich population (Bennell & Sayed, 2002b; Liang, 2002). These findings are consistent with recent results on private schools in India, Tanzania, the Philippines, and Zimbabwe (E. Jimenez & Sawada, 2001; Lassibille, et al., 2000; Machingaidze, et al., 1998; Tooley, 2000, 2001, 2002, 2003). Cheng (1999) also reported that South East Asian countries (Malaysia, Singapore, Korea, Thailand) have attempted to boost the development of their educational services through private provision to meet the growing diverse needs of citizens.

MARKET-DRIVEN EDUCATION AND RESOURCES

The expansion of the private sector in secondary education creates a market driven education system with the potential to improve educational quality through competition (Bollen, 1996; Chubb & Moe, 1990; Sanders, 2002b; Tooley, Dixon, & Stanfield, 2003). "In a market driven education system, schools compete with each other with efforts to enlarge their catchment areas by pleasing their clients and ensuring their educational careers" (Bollen, 1996 , p. 4). Wobmann (2000) contended that, "increased competition from the private schools should also have a positive effect on the effectiveness of resource use in nearby public schools" (p.18).

Furthermore, Cox and Jimenez (1997) found that private schools offer a student achievement advantage. That is, students in relatively comparable settings and conditions perform much better in private schools, at least in Colombia and Tanzania (Cox & Jimenez, 1997). Jimenez and Sawada (2001) studied the relationship between public and private schools in the Philippines found that average test scores for private schools exceeded those for public schools. However, market forces do not necessarily always lead to the improvement of educational quality, as Janssens & Leeuw (2001) indicated:

> Some individual school can decide to offer socially relevant but financially unattractive courses; other schools may start fashionable courses based on market forces, and this might lead to an imbalance in supply and demand; there are certain risks involved with variety. There is considerable tension between requirements and expectations, the available resources and the capacities on the one hand and the realization of a good education on the other (p. 46).

These tensions can result in what Janssens and his colleague referred to as "undesirable variety or variety based on powerlessness or poverty. Schools can choose to offer fewer courses, employ unqualified teachers, send classes home early, or introduce selective intake to make education more attractive to teachers" (Janssens & Leeuw, 2001, p. 46). Other empirical evidence shows that private schools tend to use more part-time teachers and sometimes those who are less qualified (Bennell & Sayed, 2002b; Fuller, 1987; Sanders, 2002b). These practices may undermine the quality of educational services offered by schools, resulting in poor school performance.

Another challenge of a market driven education system is that it might exclude "individuals or groups of individuals because they cannot buy what they need or because society cannot provide work suitable for their capabilities" (Bollen, 1996 , p. 5). Furthermore, Tsang (2002) indicated that "families with more resources have more choice than families with less resources" (p.131) to send their children to either a private school or public school. Thus, in an oddly paradoxical way, market-driven private schooling may lead to depriving some individuals or groups access to appropriate secondary education opportunities. Yet most educationists and educational organizations have asserted that educational opportunity is a basic human right (CIDA, 2002; UNESCO, 1994, 2001, 2003a). Further debate for or against market driven education is beyond the scope of this dissertation.

Government-aided Secondary Schools and Resources

In general, government-aided secondary schools have the advantage in terms of resources over private schools. Figure 3.6 clearly illustrates that both government-aided and partly government-aided secondary schools have higher overall average numbers of teachers compared to private secondary schools, irrespective of school location (Liang, 2002). Unlike the majority of private schools, government-aided schools mainly serve middle-income and upper-income families that can afford to compete for the few places available in those schools. Also, majority of the government-aided secondary schools are old, well established, prestigious, and highly selective (Holsinger, et al., 2001).

Selective Secondary School

The most selective schools in Uganda are comprised of the older, established and prestigious government-aided secondary schools. These traditionally selective schools in Uganda have more access to critical resources and offer more comprehensive curriculum (K. M. Lewin, 2001b; Liang, 2002). Empirical evidence shows that attending a selective school heavily influences success in state-level examinations at all levels because selective schools tend to have better staff and better facilities (Papas & Psacharopoulos, 1991b; Spady, 1976).

According to Liang (2002), selective schools not only tend to do better on examinations because they are better furnished with resources, but are better managed. Papas and Psacharopoulos (1991b) found that because selective schools give comprehensive entry examinations, traditionally disadvantaged groups of students are prevented from joining those schools. These authors found that male students were more likely to be admitted and to attend a selective school than girls. Therefore the selectivity in secondary schools has fundamental equity implications (Holsinger & Cowell, 2000; Little, 2000), and effectively promotes social inequity (Papas & Psacharopoulos, 1991b).

An extremely competitive education system tends to favor the best students, in term of academic ability, to enter the best schools (based on performance on public examinations) while the weak students end up in struggling schools (Lam, Wong, & Ho, 2002; Little, 2000).

This creates a "cycle of inequality" that is very difficult to escape, and functionally traps less able (socially and financially) students from getting ahead through educational avenues.

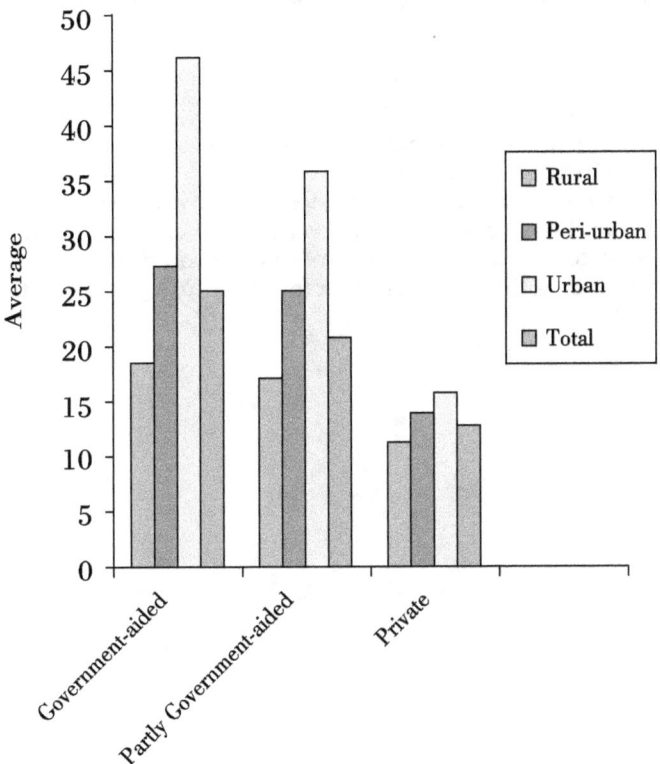

Figure 3.6. Teachers per School by School Type and by Location in 2000.4

Whether superior critical resources possessed by the selective schools influence their superior performance needs to be investigated. Whether better performance in selective schools has more to do with the fact that students attending them are screened and therefore enter with more ability, than the fact that the schools simply possess critical resources, remains unclear.

Boarding Versus Day Secondary Schools

In general, boarding secondary schools require more resources and facilities than day schools. In addition, boarding secondary schools cost more (Fuller & Clarke, 1994), so disadvantaged groups of youth cannot afford to gain access to many of the more selective boarding schools. Consequently, access to secondary education is greatly skewed to benefit the already advantaged; who have access to good quality primary schools, infra-structural support for learning, and better resourced family backgrounds (K. M. Lewin, 2001b). Lewin (2001) reported boarding traditions (unprecedented tendencies of parents and their students in opting for boarding schools) at secondary level are well established and are generally the preferred delivery provision in developing countries. There are very few contemporary studies dealing with performance differences between day and boarding schools in developing countries (Fuller, 1987; Thias & Carnoy, 1972).

CONCLUSION

Secondary education plays a pivotal role in the life of the world's children, since they join secondary schools as children and they leave as young adults. Therefore secondary education socializes the children into responsible and productive citizens. This chapter has highlighted that unprecedented expansion of private education at secondary school level. Given that school resources and school performance are critical to the school's survival—and entirely depends upon its performance on the public examinations. Chapter four presents addresses this issue.

CHAPTER FOUR

STATUS OF SCHOOL PERFORMANCE, PUBLIC EXAMINATION AND RESOURCES

School quality and performance are quite often linked to examination results (Kellaghan & Greaney, 1992; Lloyd, et al., 2003; Mortimore, 1991). School resources are vital in promoting the enabling environment for students to achieve better examination results. A recent study in Greece revealed that better resourced schools performed higher on the public examinations than poorly resourced schools (Papas & Psacharopoulos, 1991b). Bennell and Sayed (2002b) indicated that the best performing secondary schools also tend to have relatively low unit costs because they usually have larger student enrollment than poorly performing schools.

Furthermore, Wobmann (2000) found a "strong positive link between centralized examinations and student performance" (p. 13). He observed that students increasingly learn to make better use of their own resources to invest in their education, such as devoting their time and attention (Wobmann, 2000). It is also important to note that administering public examinations requires incredible amounts of resources and efforts in order to improve and maintain the examination quality. This is a worthwhile investment given the role of examinations in any given education system. Kellaghan & Greaney (1992) also underscored the fact that quality public examinations positively influence what is being taught in schools and, in turn, foster improvement in the quality of education. Thus, lack of critical resources may undermine the quality and the usefulness of public examinations in developing countries (Kellaghan & Greaney, 1992).

While examination results may play a significant role in the selectivity of students, most education system in developing countries such as Uganda, have tended to over emphasize examination results. This challenge is compounded even further by the fact that the selection of candidates for admission into either post-secondary institutions or business organizations for employment, are based almost exclusively on public examination results. Therefore, schools are challenged to produce better examination results all the time in order to survive the competition. In this competitive climate, schools are forced to devote much more attention and efforts on activities intended to improve their examination results (S. Kajubi, 1992; Kim, 2001; Little, 2000). Bauer, Brust, and Hubbert (2002) reported similar experience in Kenya's education system.

Interestingly, once schools achieve excellence in performance in public examinations, parents and their students begin to struggle to gain admission into those best performing schools. As such those excelling schools in public examinations tend to gain and enjoy more student enrollment than their counterparts. Quite often poorly performing schools instead tend to lose students as they transfer to the best performing schools (J. M. Hite, Hite, Mugimu, et al., 2004). It is not surprising therefore that many students, teachers, and parents may indulge in examination mal-practices in order to improve their grades at all cost (S. Kajubi, 1992; Nsubuga, 2004). Consequently, examination mal-practices may compromise the quality of education.

Teaching to the test is not an uncommon phenomenon (Papas & Psacharopoulos, 1991b; Sanders, 2002b). Mortimore (1991) reported similar experiences with public examinations in the British education system. Unfortunately, the over-emphasis on examination results does not necessarily translate into higher pass rates or better grades and improved school quality (Harber & Davies, 1997). However, most schools continue to coach and drill their students preparing them for the national examinations. This is not only unique to Uganda but also many other countries. Papas and Psacharopoulos (1991b) study in Greece revealed that "nearly three out of four students, in their sample, attended cram school either under individual instruction or in a class with a group of other students" (p. 407).

Nonetheless, the use of public examination results, as a measure of school performance as well as a benchmark for informing numerous policy decisions affecting education remains paradoxical. This is mainly due to the inconsistent practices occurring during the process of handling and administering public examinations to students. Inconsistent practice may include allowing private candidates and repeaters to be examined from their school examination centers, hiring university students to take examinations on behalf of candidates, over-drilling students on test taking skills, consequently, our ability to discern the effects of school resources on school performance may be confounded. However, education policy analysts throughout the developing world have sought to use public examination scores as one of the key tools to measure and evaluate school quality. Yet, most developing countries may lack critical evaluative resources such as national examinations of good quality to do so.

PUBLIC EXAMINATION AS A MEASURE OF EDUCATIONAL QUALITY

It is a widely accepted belief that student outcome that is cognitive achievement is a product of school quality and can be measured by public examinations. Murnane (1981) indicated that public examinations provide superior measures of student achievement at the national level. Lockheed and Hanushek (1988) also contended "the underlying requirement in measuring [school] effectiveness and in evaluating potential policies is the identification of a given set of inputs that have homogeneous relationship with student outcomes (p. 28)." In this respect the national examination results have been used to measure and evaluate the quality of schooling world over (Mortimore, 1991). The rationale behind administering public examinations is to develop, score, report, and evaluate the performance of schools, teachers, and students unambiguously (M. Lockheed & E. Hanushek, 1988). Developing countries, such as Uganda, may administer public examinations to compare achievement across regions, districts, counties, schools, and within schools (Wobman, 2000). In addition, it would be in common place for the government, politicians, policy makers, and the Ministry of Education to use public examination results/scores to judge the quality and effectiveness of schools for purposes of determining what schools should receive particular services. It is questionable whether better public examination scores obtained by a school may necessarily suggest better/superior education services provided for children attending such schools.

In a study covering 13 Latin American countries, Willms and Somers (2001) concluded that the most effective schools frequently administered tests to their pupils. In Uganda also examinations, whether at the national, district, or school level, are an important school resource and play a significant role in improving the quality of schools (J. M. Hite, Hite, Rew, Mugimu, & Nsubuga, 2003).

Judging the quality of schools based on public examination results is highly criticized for the tendency to over look existing differences among schools in terms of student characteristics they serve, unfair allocation of resources, etc. (Kellaghan & Greaney, 2001). In addition, according to Lockheed and Hanushek (1988), because of the large and diverse curriculums at higher levels of education, such as secondary education, it becomes difficult to construct public examinations that can be used to accurately and objectively measure the quality of education for all types of schools and for all students (Willms & Somers, 2001).

Although national examinations have limitations, many think that public examinations could positively contribute to improving school quality and student performance. Wobmann (2000) reported that where centrally controlled public examinations are administered, schools, teachers, students and parents are more in tune to improve students' performance. He also argues that "given the central [public] examinations, the leeway of teachers to act opportunistically is reduced and the incentives to use resources more effectively are increased...[and] thus, a strong positive link between centralized public examinations and student performance" (p. 13). Furthermore, Kellaghan & Greaney (1992) suggest that public examination of good quality could be important tools to influence what is being taught in school and in turn foster considerable improvements in the quality of education. Yet, critical lack of resources in many developing countries may undermine the quality and the usefulness of public examinations (Kellaghan & Greaney, 1992). However, in the context of developing countries, examination scores remain one of the most reliable and valid ways to compare and evaluate schools (Wobmann, 2000).

PUBLIC EXAMINATION IN UGANDA

Taking the case of Uganda, its education system is well known in Sub-Saharan Africa for its commitment to public examinations. However, the authorities in the Ministry of Education and Sports have not adequately optimized the use of public examination results in their planning for improving educational quality at different levels of the education system. For example, Bennell & Sayed (2002) stated that UCE and UACE results have not been systematically analyzed. However, recognizing that public examination can only be useful if they are of good quality, thus, the quality issues of Ugandan public examinations need to be assessed. In recent years, research evidence shows that results on UCE and UACE examinations has declined (Bennell & Sayed, 2002a). Lewin (2002) asserts that there should be analysis of UCE and UACE test scores between public and private schools in Uganda, especially in the attempt to examine the status of public examinations in Uganda as well as the implications of public examinations on the system.

Public Examinations: A National Policy Makers' Perspective

In Uganda, public examinations play the selectivity role and indeed influence the admission decisions at secondary education and post-secondary education levels (P. W. S. Kajubi, 1992). Thus, the quality of schools is profoundly judged based on their public examination results (Kellaghan & Greaney, 1992). The best schools are usually announced over the national radio, television, and also published in the government newspapers. The quality of school ranges from the best selective schools to the very poor schools for both government-aided and private schools (Holsinger & Cowell, 2000) as based on their public examination results or scores. School administrators, teachers and students tend to be pressured for producing better results in public examinations. Consequently, teachers may tend to focus only on examinable subject content and may ignore the rest. The Government White Paper reported:

> The deliberate neglect by students, teachers and schools, of vital subjects which are not examined and the development of the tendencies of drilling, coaching and commercializing private tuition, and their consequent detrimental effects on the mental, moral, and ethical development of students, let alone the heavy financial burdens all this imposes on parents (P. W. S. Kajubi, 1992, p. 82).

The tendency to over-emphasize public examination results in Ugandan schools has led to unintended consequences. That is, it is not uncommon for some students, teachers, and parents to indulge in examination mal-practices, which potentially undermine the quality of education. Teaching to the test is also not an uncommon phenomenon (Papas & Psacharopoulos, 1991a; Sanders, 2002a). Peter Mortimore (1991) reports a similar experience in the British education system as a result of over-emphasis on public examination results. Yet, placing too much emphasis on public examination results does not necessarily translate into higher grades or scores (Harber & Davies, 1997).

The Ministry of Education and Sports oversees the quality of examinations by monitoring the activities of the national examining body. The Uganda National Examination Board (UNEB) is a government parastatal responsible for setting and marking public examinations. UNEB is also responsible for training the personnel involved in developing and scoring examinations. These include examiners and markers selected from the pool of practicing teachers working in various schools across the country. UNEB provides national public examinations at the end of each education cycle. That is, primary leaving examinations (UPE) at the end of the seven year primary cycle, Uganda certificate of education (UCE) at the end of fourth year in secondary education and Uganda advanced certificate of education (UACE) at the end of the two years of advanced level secondary education. At each exit level, UNEB issues formal certificates to successful candidates to acknowledge their academic achievements, which credentials may be useful in securing employment or qualifying for further training (Kellaghan & Greaney, 1992).

Lewin (2002) reports that the Ugandan secondary school system is outdated and overloaded, and predominantly focuses on public examination and certification in shaping learning and teaching outcomes. For instance, Lewin (2002) reports that "half or more secondary level students fail to reach criteria referenced levels of achievement in core subjects" (p.5). Recognizing the rapidly increasing growth of the secondary education sector the challenge of deteriorating standards in public examinations may be magnified even further with the current scarce resources (Liang, 2002).

EXAMINATION FORMAT

The public examinations take on the form of multiple-type, structured-type, and written essay-type questions [that theory-driven] depending on the subject. For some subjects, candidates have to take either the practical or oral exams in addition to the theory papers.

Table 4.1. Subject grading criteria for UCE and UACE

Exam Level	Distinctions (Above Average)	Credits (Average)	Passes (Below Average)	Fail (Poor)
UCE (O -Level)	D1 & D2	C3, C4, C5, & C6	P7 & P8	F9
	Principle Pass	Subsidiary Pass	Pass	Fail
UACE (A -Level)	A, B, C, D, &E	O	P7 & P8	F9

Table 4.1 shows that for UCE examination scores are graded based on distinctions, credits, passes and fail while at UACE level grading is done base on principle passes and subsidiary passes.

Table 4.2. Aggregate grading criteria for UCE and UACE.

Exam Level	Criteria
UCE	
Division. 1 (Highest)	A credit in English, math, and one science and < 23 points
Division 2	< 32 aggregated points and below
Division 3	Between 32-44 aggregated points
Division 4	Between 45-53 aggregated points
Division. 9 (Lowest)	54 and above aggregated points
UACE	
Result 5 (Pass)	At least 3 passes
9 (Fail)	

Table 4.2. Shows common grading system for Ugandan secondary national examinations. For UCE, overall grading falls under four categories or divisions 1-4 constituting an aggregated score. Division 1 or first grade is determined based on the best-done six subjects totaling to 23 aggregated points and below. Table 4.2 also presents other criteria for determining the type of grade. For instance, a candidate at UCE level to achieve grade one must obtain at least a credit in the following subjects: English language or any other language, Biology, and Mathematics. Furthermore, It is important to note that majority of UCE candidates find it extremely

difficult to pass in division one since most of them do not pass English, Biology and Mathematics. That is, these subjects are poorly done because it is difficult to find qualified teachers to teach them particularly in the rural areas, lack of laboratory facilities, and shortage of textbooks (Liang, 2002; Nsubuga, 2004).

GENERAL IMPLICATIONS OF PUBLIC EXAMINATIONS FOR STUDENTS

College entry: Examination results are central in determining whether a student qualifies for college entrance. Moreover, there are very few places at post secondary /tertiary levels therefore candidates must score very high in the public examination in order to be admitted to these institutions. For instance, only 10 percent of secondary school graduates enter the university or technical and commercial colleges (Nsubuga, 2004). Examination results are not only important for the student to progress academically but also for employment opportunities. It is not uncommon for students to repeat "A" level several times for them to be able to obtain enough grades either to enable them join tertiary education or to secure employment. When students repeat several times it is a waste of resources on part of the students and the parents and it raises their financial burden. Indeed many students may give up along the way before completing the academic cycle.

Vocational training: Most schools have neglected subjects related to vocational training. Recognizing that vocational subjects are extremely costly and the teachers qualified to teach vocational subjects are also difficult to find. Thus, with over-burdened budgets, most schools cannot afford to offer vocational subjects, as these subjects are so demanding in terms of instructional resources such as workshop equipments, tools, and materials for practical activities required in teaching and practical examinations. It is not surprising that vocational, scientific, and technological oriented subjects are offered to very few students (less than a third or 30 percent) compared to those that offer humanities and other related subjects (K. Lewin, 2002). Generally, students fail Mathematics and Science subjects compared to humanities such as History and Religious Studies.

Why do exams matter for students? Examination results help students to progress from one level to the next. Public examination results may certainly determine the fate of most students, in terms of whether the students will be able to move on or progress from one educational level to the next, or join the job market.

It is not uncommon for head teachers of some schools to misuse examination fees collected from students and each year a few candidates may miss their examinations. An examination fee is a huge financial burden to majority of disadvantaged groups and many of them miss examinations as a result of their failure to pay. In addition, students that fail to pay examination fees are denied access to take public examinations, thus loosing all the years of schooling. Of the students who registered for UCE during the five years period 1999 to 2003, 5.7 percent on average missed their public examinations (Nsubuga, 2004). Furthermore, students attending schools that have no recognized examination centers cover additional cost to other schools and are required to pay additional expenses towards their transportation, accommodation, and feeding during the public examination period.

Chapter 4 - Status of School Performance, Public Examination and Resources

Implications of Public Examinations for Schools: A Practitioner's Perspective

Each school administrator, in any Ugandan national examination center school will agree that the external pressure for better public examination results often gets beyond control. School administrators are forced to allocate more of the school's meager financial resources as a primary strategy of preparing candidates for excellence in public examinations. That is, extra resources are dedicated towards hiring experts in the teaching profession such as examiners and markers. Examiners and markers are engaged to coach and drill the candidates especially giving them tips on how to take the public examinations.

It is the role of the school administrator to ensure that his/her school provides adequate security during public examinations, to safeguard their schools from malpractices. Otherwise schools indulging in such activities are usually disqualified by UNEB. School administrators also ensure that all public examinations done each day are returned to the local police station where they are kept in safe custody, until UNEB officials deliver them to the head office from where they are distributed to various marking centers.

FINANCING EXAMINATIONS

Big portions of the school budgets go to supporting administration of public examinations. Although, parents and students are required to meet the expenses of public examinations through designated examination fees charged based on the number of subjects and level of education of the candidate, the school has to meet additional costs of transportation of exams, providing examination seats [that meet the required standard of UNEB], creating examination rooms, laboratory and laboratory equipments. Thus, the whole process of administering public examinations is extremely costly for both the parent and the school. The schools preparing candidate classes without examination centers collaborate with other schools with centers to allow their students to take public examinations there. However, the schools without public examination centers pay much more additional costs than the rest of the students in order to take their public examinations from other schools. Therefore, parents prefer those schools with examination centers. Thus, the possession of an examination center creates an added advantage for the schools.

EXAMINATION STRATEGIES AT THE SCHOOL LEVEL

Different schools use a variety of strategies to prepare candidates for taking national examinations and ensuring that their candidates can excel in the public examinations. Some of the strategies commonly used by most schools include:

1) Selecting only those candidates who are capable of passing and excluding/eliminating weak ones who are incapable of passing.
2) Schools and parents organize coaching programs—allocating extra time after normal school hours [at night, on weekends, and during holidays] for offering extra help to students.
3) Rewarding teachers for excellence, those whose students excel in their subject in public examinations are given special recognition and sometimes receive increments in their allowances.

4) Sharing internal examinations and external joint mock examinations organized at district or regional levels and administering frequent internal assessment tests to candidate classes.

5) Schools may share teachers with special expertise such examiners to mentor their students and preparing candidates how to take the public examinations.

6) Schools organize joint seminars for candidate classes where students from various schools meet to discuss important topics under the guidance of experts in the subject.

IMPLICATIONS OF PUBLIC EXAMINATIONS

The essence of going to school becomes "passing examinations". So the notion of learning basic skills as required by the content of the curriculum ceases to be the priority. Rote memorization of the testable items is the preferred approach than enhancing problem solving skills. Otherwise teachers, students, administrators, and parents may just focus on examinable materials to help students learn how to excel in public examinations. The costs attached to this emphasis on getting good public examinations results are too great that the financial costs and undue pressures on students, parents, and school administration sometimes becomes unbearable.

The public examination may have equity implications because students who are financially and socially advantaged usually do better in public examinations than their counterparts the disadvantaged ones. Since advantaged students usually attend better primary schools and gain enormous support from their parents and guardians,, they receive better quality education and guidance, which boosts their subsequent performance at post primary education levels. Consequently, advantaged students are more likely to join the elite selective schools rather than to their counterparts. It is evident that majority of disadvantaged groups attend the struggling schools in the rural areas that virtually lack most of the basic resources (Bennell & Sayed, 2002a).

It is important to note that schools that are excelling in public examinations will gain more students while poor schools will loose theirs. Indeed, all those students whose parents can afford to pay are likely to move on to the best performing schools. These trends have serious policy implications, for instance many struggling schools may close due to lack of students. Indeed each year many schools close.

Use of Public Examination Results for National Level Educational Planning

Kelleghan & Greaney (2001) indicates that Ugandan district education authorities attempted to improve classroom strategies basing on information derived from national assessment carried out by UNEB [p. 57]. They organized a series of workshops and seminars for teacher trainers, school inspectors, and teachers in which the results from assessments were presented (Kelleghan & Greaney, 2001)[p. 57]. Nsubuga (2004) argued that since "examinations have been used to evaluate the curriculum, teachers, learners and school programs, the candidates performance makes the stakeholders raise questions about the school leadership" (p.6). Therefore, it is national policy that as soon as examination results are released by UNEB, they are published in newspapers, announced on radio and television (TV) for public consumption. Then the public is able to compare the performance of schools based

Chapter 4 - Status of School Performance, Public Examination and Resources

on the examination results. University selections are also based on the examination results of candidates.

CONCLUSION

We have seen how public examinations drive and influence the curriculum, with reference to what teachers teach in schools. Public examinations promote selectivity. Schools are measured basing on their performance on the public examinations. It is not surprising that school managers dedicate more and more meager school resources towards students' preparations for the public examinations. Resources contributing towards better grades in public examinations are taken seriously. Chapter six presents the research questions and methods of the study.

CHAPTER FIVE

METHODOLOGY

The methods we chose to use were meant to address the research problem that very little is known about the role of school resources on school performance at the secondary level in developing countries (Hanushek, 1995; Scheerens, 2001a). Thus, policy makers are limited in making informed, but difficult, decisions on how to distribute resources to improve the quality of secondary education (UNESCO, 2001). Therefore, there is pressing need for further research to explore the relationship between school resources and secondary school performance in the context of developing countries.

Therefore, this study examined whether schools endowed with greater levels of critical resources consistently outperform others. This study focused on exploring relationships between school resources (physical, human, financial, contextual) and school performance as measured by Ugandan National Examination Board (UNEB) aggregated UCE scores in secondary schools in Mukono Uganda. This study has contributed to literature by utilizing the Resource-Based View logic to interpret the findings. This is the first study of its kind to offer this new way of interpreting and understanding the relationships between school resources and school performance based on RBV logic. Six central questions motivated this research:

1. What demographic and contextual school factors are critical for secondary school performance in Mukono Uganda?
2. What is the current status of resources in secondary schools in Mukono Uganda?
3. What are the relationships between financial resources and performance in secondary schools in Mukono Uganda?
4. What are the relationships between physical resources and performance in secondary schools in Mukono Uganda?
5. What are the relationships between human resources and performance in secondary schools in Mukono Uganda?
6. How is the combination of all three types of resources (financial, physical, and human) related to school performance in secondary schools in Mukono Uganda?

This chapter presents the variables and the theoretical conceptual model of the study. This chapter first highlights the hypotheses. Secondly, the chapter presents the dependent, independent, and control variables in the research model and the rationale underlying each variable's inclusion in the model (Munro, 2001a). Thirdly, the chapter identifies the proposed research design of the study and focuses on the methodology, instrumentation, and data collection. Fourthly, the chapter describes the four data sets gathered from Mukono district in Uganda. Finally, a brief explanation of the statistical procedures is presented.

RESOURCE MODEL, HYPOTHESES AND VARIABLES

Figure 5.1 summarizes the conceptual model utilized to examine the research questions. In general, the model proposed that three different categories of resources—financial, physical and human—should have a positive influence on the performance of secondary schools. The primary motivation of this research was to demonstrate to what extent these resources explained school performance in Mukono, Uganda. Thus, the research model in Figure 5.1, which suggested the seven hypotheses, guided this study.

Hypotheses

Financial resources are the monetary assets of an organization. Financial resources represent a school's fluid or tangible resources that is, they can easily be transformed into other strategic resources (Bienayme, 1995) such as physical and human resources. Financial resources can be used in purchasing new textbooks, science equipment and hiring more skilled teachers that can facilitate student-learning outcomes. Consequently, schools charging lower fees (having limited access to financial resources) may generally tend to also suffer from lack of other educational resources (Bauer, et al., 2002). Thus, access to more financial resources may boost school performance.

Hypothesis 1   Secondary schools in Mukono Uganda with more financial resources will perform higher in examination scores than other schools.

Critical physical resources are likely to facilitate conducive academic learning environments that should contribute positively to student outcomes (McGuffey, 1982). Furthermore, critical physical resources are not only likely to facilitate a positive academic learning atmosphere, but also could attract the best-qualified teachers and highly motivated students as well (Fuller, 1987). The best-qualified teachers may perhaps prefer to teach in well-facilitated schools. Likewise, parents of highly motivated students may also prefer to enroll their students in elite schools that have adequate critical physical resources. Therefore better quality critical physical resources may boost students' learning outcomes.

Hypothesis 2   Secondary schools in Mukono Uganda with more physical resources will perform higher in examination scores than other schools.

The quality and quantity of critical human resources, such as highly qualified teachers, are the primary resources in facilitating student-learning outcomes, particularly in developing countries (Murnane, 1981). Furthermore, experienced administrators, through the effective management of schools, are able to create a positive learning environment and therefore contribute to better student learning outcomes (Fullan, 1997).

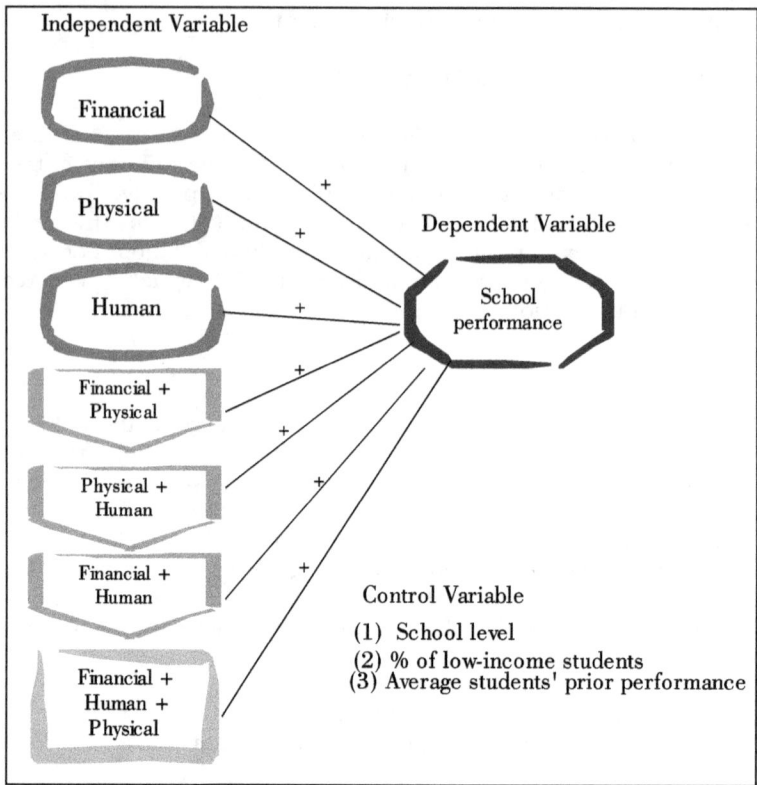

Figure 5.1 Model of School Resources and School Performance

Hypothesis 3 Secondary schools in Mukono Uganda with more human resources will perform higher in examination scores than other schools.

Access to higher levels of financial resources may lead to more physical resources, creating a more positive educational learning environment. For instance, extra financial resources can be used to acquire new technologies such as computers for the school. "Computers can break down barriers of schooling enabling students and teachers to participate in virtual learning across the world, where there is almost instant access to almost limitless information and where physical space is no longer a limit to learning" (Hargreaves & Fullan, 1998, p. 74-5). The "use of technology can deepen, extend, and invigorate student's learning" (Hargreaves & Fullan, 1998, p. 76).

Hypothesis 4 Secondary schools in Mukono Uganda with more both financial and physical resources will perform higher in examination scores than other schools.

A combination of higher physical resources and human resources could indicate secondary schools with people/staff who could more effectively and efficiently utilize physical resources to gain a competitive advantage (Mugimu & Hite, 2001). This competitive advantage in turn could lead to higher school performance.

Hypothesis 5   Secondary schools in Mukono Uganda with more of both physical and human resources will perform higher in examination scores than other schools.

Access to both financial and human resources can lead to superior school performance. Why? Because teachers can be facilitated in their work by providing them with instructional materials they need to become more effective in their work. Having financial resources alone is not enough, if schools lack qualified human resources. Conversely, a school having the best-qualified teachers without motivating them is self-defeating. Schools find it hard to attract and retain these highly qualified teachers without having such resources.

Teachers feel job insecurity where non-payment affects their morale. Note that however qualified the teachers may be, if they are not paid, they may lose morale and this negatively affects student performance (Chapman & Mulkeen, 2003; Fullan & Hargreaves, 1996; Harber & Davies, 1997). Conversely, in systems where teachers' salaries are paid promptly, they may enjoy job security and may be more committed to their work, hence, schools may perform better. Yet, in developing countries delayed payment and non-payment of teachers' salaries is a huge problem.

Hypothesis 6   Secondary schools in Mukono Uganda with more financial- and human resources will perform higher in examination scores than other schools.

Lastly, schools endowed with all the three different kinds of critical resources--financial, physical, and human will be able to conceive of and implement many different vital educational programs that could and should improve student learning outcomes. That is, schools having greater access to a variety of critical resources could have greater flexibility in implementing and providing a variety of strategic unique educational services (Barney, 1991a) that could promote superior performance.

Hypothesis 7.   Secondary schools in Mukono Uganda with more of all resources combined (human, financial, and physical) will perform highest in examination scores than other schools.

DEPENDENT VARIABLE

The dependent variable in this study was school performance. The average aggregated UCE examination scores were used as a proxy indicator for measuring school performance. The performance of secondary school students in Mukono Uganda in UCE examination scores ranges between four passing grades (divisions 1-4) and one failing grade (i.e. F 9). Division 1 is the highest and F9 is the lowest. School-level performance was obtained by computing the average UCE exam score for each school.

It is important to note that though the use of examination scores to evaluate school performance is highly contested, it is the best available, reliable, and valid indicator that is universally acceptable in most developing countries (M. E. Lockheed & E. A. Hanushek, 1988). Therefore, the study used average UCE examination scores despite various theoretical and empirical challenges to employing only a single variable of school performance (Capon, Farley, & Hoenig, 1990; Durand, 1999; Rouse & Daellensbach, 2002; Venkatraman & Ramanujam, 1986).

INDIPENDENT VARIABLES

The predictors used in this research fell under three main categories of financial, physical, and human resource variables. Given the high number of resource variables in the collected data, the independent variables chosen to represent these three categories were selected, basing on the initial finding of their positive association with school performance, specifically in terms of national UCE examination scores.

FINANCIAL RESOURCES

Financial capital is the stock of fungible and tangible assets [money] upon which the school can draw. Financial capital can translate into the physical components of a school, such as classrooms, and instructional materials (Hill & Guthrie, 1999). Financial capital is essential for a school to function as a true organization. Some schools may have a wider range of financial resource sources than others, which could influence their performance. Six financial resource variables were included in the analysis.

School revenue: This variable is the square root of total school revenue in 2002-2003. The researcher computed the square root of total school revenue to reduce the outlier effect among schools. School revenue was generated from students' school fees and represented the extent of liquid assets that could be used to exchange for other critical resources. Schools with more funds are likely to implement educational programs that could lead to better performance. For instance, richer schools can afford to make available a sufficient number of computers with Internet connection, thus providing opportunities for additional references and educational resources via the Internet.

Filing revenue reports: This variable reports a dummy variable coded 1 if the school filed revenue reports to the government. Filing revenue reports was a proxy for effective financial management and accountability. This may perhaps free up additional financial resources that could be used to create additional educational services to boost school performance.

Value of past loans: This variable measures the value of past loans. Securing loans provides financial leverage, which could be translated into critical school resources for implementing strategic educational programs to improve student learning outcomes. Furthermore, loan funds could be used to create additional infrastructure needed to improve the learning environment of the school.

Government support: Government-aided secondary schools generally have greater access to government funding sources than private schools (for instance Capitation Grants (CG), Capital Development Funds (CDF), donations and teachers' salaries). This variable measures the amount of government funding support the school received.

Extent of government support: This variable measures the square root/ percentage of school government support over total school revenue. The total government support was the sum of all monies contributed to the school by the state in terms of CG, CDF, donations, and teacher salaries. These funds were accumulated for the fiscal year June 2002 to June 2003.

PHYSICAL RESOURCES

Physical resources (sometimes known as physical capital) are tangible resources, which may include school buildings, geographic location, science equipments, computers, and other instructional materials (Barney, 2002; Grant, 1991). Physical resources are important components that could contribute to organizational performance. Eight physical resource variables found to show the strongest correlation with dependent variable were included in the analysis.

Library use: This variable was a dummy variable coded 1 if students actually use the library and zero if students did not use the library. Availability of a well-stocked library without students actually utilizing its facilities may not translate into student learning outcomes.

Book-student ratio: This variable denoted the total number of books divided by total student enrollment. Many schools suffer from an inadequate supply of textbooks, and textbooks are usually costly. Therefore, for many schools their strained financial budgets did not enable schools to acquire sufficient textbooks and instructional materials. Students attending a school with a higher books / student ratio were likely to perform better, because such students could do much more in terms of self-directed learning/study beyond what the teachers offer in the classroom.

Flush toilets: This variable was defined as the ratio of students having access to flush toilet facilities. Flush toilets are resources that are valuable, rare, and difficult to copy. Most schools could not afford to duplicate this resource. Richer parents and their children might prefer schools that offer better hygienic conditions. Better-qualified teachers might also prefer to work for schools that offer a clean environment schools with flush toilets provided. Availability of flush toilets created better hygienic conditions that perhaps attracted better-qualified teachers and academically more able students hence might boost school performance.

Internet connection: This variable was a dummy variable coded 1 if the school administration has access to an Internet connection. The Internet is a cutting edge way of accessing and sharing numerous kinds of information quickly and reliably, hence provides better performance advantage to schools connected to the worldwide web (Hargreaves & Fullan, 1998). A school connected to the Internet would have greater access to "internet-based sources of learning materials and information" (K. M. Lewin, 2000, p. 19) that might facilitate better students' outcomes. Such schools could leverage their resources with other institutions across the world.

Science laboratory: This variable was defined as students' use of the science laboratory based on the average number of hours per week. A school laboratory could be an important component in learning science, depending upon the degree to which it is efficiently and effectively utilized. The availability of a science laboratory alone does not necessarily mean that students will do well in science, however, particularly if the students and teachers are not actually using the science laboratory facilities optimally (K. M. Lewin, 2000).

Buildings with glass: This variable was defined as the ratio of building with glass windows and doors. The appearance of school buildings matters because it might attract parents and students into a certain school. Buildings with glass windows and doors could offer a better learning environment by allowing more light in from outside of the buildings (Lyons, 2001). Furthermore, "natural light has profound influence on the [human] body and mind" (Lyons, 2001, p. 3). Glass window buildings also improve the appearance of the school, making it attractive for the parents and students. They are sign of permanence, since they cannot be used in semi permanent or temporary buildings. The use of glass is a sign of the seriousness school management invests in physical resources. Buildings without glass windows are usually dark, dull, and offer a miserable learning environment. Parents and student would prefer attractive schools.

Electric power: This variable was a dummy variable, coded 1 if the school has regular electric power supply. In the context of developing countries, being connected to the main electric power supply is not a guarantee that electricity will always be available. It is not uncommon for a school to spend months without electricity. A regular power supply denotes having electricity most of the time, even if it sometimes goes out. Indeed some schools provide generators as an alternative power source to fill in when electricity goes out. Students will learn better in classrooms with sufficient and predictable lighting provisions.

Entertainment facilities: This variable was defined as the ratio of available rooms for potential entertainment such as the main hall, examination rooms and dining halls. In secondary schools in Uganda, entertainment is often in form of disco dances, movie shows, television shows, debates, drama, and music shows staged by fellow students. Such extra-curricular activities allow the students time out of the rigorous classroom activities to relax, free their minds from worry, which might contribute to better students' outcomes.

HUMAN RESOURCES

Human resources (sometimes known as human capital) include people-based skills, experiences, relationships, innovation, and creativity of people (Barney, 2002; Grant, 1991). According to Grant (1991), "human resources are the most strategically important resources of an organization" (p. 119). Six human resource variables were included in the analysis.

Teacher examiners: This variable was the percentage of teachers in each school who are specialized in setting standardized national examinations. Teacher examiners receive special training from UNEB on how to set and to mark national examinations. Thus, they gain technical skills for scoring and answering questions on the national examinations. Therefore, examiners could draw on this knowledge to teach their own students, which might boost the performance of their own students.

Teacher markers: This variable was the percentage of teachers specialized in marking standardized national examinations. Teacher markers also receive special training from UNEB for scoring national examination papers. Thus, they are exposed to technical skills in answering questions in national examination that they could draw on to guide their own students.

Student-teacher ratio: This variable was the total number of students divided by the total number of teachers in each school. Research on class size and its impact on students' outcomes particularly in both industrialized and developing countries remain equivocal (Hanushek, 1995; Willms & Somers, 2001). The optimal class size, that is the student-teacher ratio in the context of developing countries is not known.

Part-time teachers: This variable was the percentage of part-time teachers in relation to the total number of teachers in each school. Part-time teachers may not always be available to students for consultation and other academic support needed outside official classroom hours (Lassibille, Tan, & Sumra, 1998). Therefore, students attending schools with greater numbers of part-time teachers might perform poorly due to limited access to teachers. Nonetheless, schools contract specialized teachers, such as examiners, markers, and well-known experts in specific disciplines and subjects. More of these categories of teachers might enhance school performance because of their special expertise, even though they are contracted on a part-time basis.

Boarding students: This variable was the percentage of the number of boarding students to the total number of students in each school. Schools often serve both boarding and day students. In schools with more boarding students, teachers have more time to prepare students to master the curriculum and take examinations. Schools with more boarding students could perform higher on the examination scores than other schools (Fuller, 1987; Thias & Carnoy, 1972).

Female teachers: This variable was the percentage of the number of female teachers in relation to the total number of teachers in each school. Female teachers could be role models to students particularly by encouraging girls to stay in school and go on to further education (UNDP, 2002).

CONTROL VARIABLES

To appropriately test the hypotheses, the researcher included control variables for the effects of school levels, percentage of low-income students, and average prior students' performance. The variable "School level" represents whether the school offers only "O" level exams or both "O" and "A" level examinations. The school level is important in that A-level students may serve as role models to O-level students, which may influence O-level students' performance. The researcher also controlled the percentage of low-income students, as reported by the school administrators. Educational effectiveness literature underscores the notion that socio-economic status and family background contribute to the largest portion of student outcomes. Families not only provide financial resources for securing educational materials to support the child's education, but also social capital in terms of parental education, siblings' ability to teach and help with studies, and access to community resources provided through family social relationships that could contribute fundamentally to students' educational achievement (Coleman & Hoffer, 2000). The third control variable "Average prior students' performance" was measured by averaging all obtained students' scores on which admission in senior one was based. This was based on the assumption that students stay in one school to complete the four-year cycle of lower secondary education.

The initial analysis started with five potential control variables. However, after running the first regression model with all the six control variables, the researcher found only the school level, percentage of low-income students, and average prior students' performance to be statistically significant at a p-value less than 0.05. The other insignificant control variables (see Appendix D) were not included in all subsequent regression models.

Research Design

This study utilized a correlational-regression research design (Sirkin, 1995). This study was correlational in nature by virtue of exploring relationships existing between variables (Gay & Airasian, 2000; S. J. Hite, 2001; P. V. Young, 2000).

DATA COLLECTION

This study utilized archival data collected during the BYU Uganda International Volunteers Program in 2003. This section describes how this data was collected.

SAMPLE DESIGN

The sample initially included 74 schools comprising 19 government-aided and 55 private secondary schools. However, only 63 secondary schools were included in the final data regression analysis because they were the only schools in which UNEB examinations were available. Majority of sampled schools predominantly served rural and low-income student populations. Table 5.1 presents the demographic information about the sampled schools. The main criterion for selecting schools was that all schools had an UNEB examination center by 2002. The first reason for this criterion is that only UNEB schools provide annual national examination scores.
These scores could be used as a measure of school performance. The second reason for this criterion was that these schools must fulfill certain minimum standards to become nationally recognized examination centers. Therefore, schools with UNEB centers had many factors in common, which provided the opportunity to control for extraneous variance among schools while allowing us to compare schools on other critical variables.

Chapter 5 - Methodology

Table 5.1. *Secondary Schools Demographics*

	Government-aided	Private	Total
Type			
Boarding	02	06	08
Day	13	09	22
Combined (boarding & day)	04	28	32
Level			
A and O levels	13	28	41
O levels	06	15	21
Gender			
Co-educational (mixed gender)	17	42	59
Single gender	02	02	04
Has a UNEB center	19	44	63

INSTRUMENTATION

This study utilized a four-part school site resource survey administered to the 63 school administrators of secondary schools in Mukono, Uganda (see Appendix C). Each part of the survey included both open-ended and close-ended questions (P. V. Young, 2000). The first part of survey included the consent form and a 34-item questionnaire covering data related to personnel human resources including administrators, teachers, and staff resources. The second part of the survey included a 69-item questionnaire covering data related to financial and administrative human resources. The third part of the secondary survey included a 65-item questionnaire covering data related to physical resources and educational resources. The fourth part of the survey included a 10-item questionnaire collecting data/information related to student intake, UNEB examinations, and class/school timetables. Survey questionnaires were an appropriate method of data collection, not only because surveys are among the most commonly used tools to collect data (Worthen, White, Fan, & Sudweeks, 1999), but also because the survey allowed for the collection and organization of an extremely large number of quantitative data in a reasonably short time.

Pre-testing and piloting the survey:

The survey instruments were pre-tested in the field. First, the instruments were given to several school administrators in two secondary schools randomly selected from a list of secondary schools, generated from a five-kilometer radius buffer zone around the Mukono District Education Office (DEO). These administrators identified parts of the survey that were unclear, confusing, and erroneous in some way. The instruments were revised and adjusted as deemed appropriate.

Instruments were then piloted in eight randomly selected secondary schools using replacement technique from a list of all secondary schools that were not in the final sample, after which necessary revisions were made on the instruments. Thus, pretests and pilot tests offered important insights to improve the four instruments

(Bourque & Fielder, 1995). While these four instruments generated almost 600 different variables, the focus of this study was based on a narrower set of variables that represent financial resource related, physical resource related, and human resource related variables.

Survey administration:

The surveys were administered to 63 participating UNEB secondary schools in Mukono District. In each school, one to four administrators including the headmaster, deputy headmaster, or director of studies, who were responsible for the day-to-day operations of the school, provided the relevant information. Field research assistants gained access into schools by presenting two letters (see Appendix B): First, a letter of introduction from the Permanent Secretary, MOES; and second, a letter on research project background information which contained a brief description of the University, the volunteer program in Uganda, the researchers involved, past research, and the intended research.

Field research assistants delivered and administered the surveys to each school. They also observed, interviewed, and gathered supplementary information. This interview and data collection process took from two to eight hours per school, depending upon the size of the school. Larger schools took more time than smaller schools with fewer resources. At the end of each school survey administration, the field research assistant gave a gift in the form of textbooks, maps, and a certificate of recognition for each participating school as a sign for appreciation of the participants' time.

In general school administrators were receptive and cooperative with our field research assistant in providing the information we needed. Nonetheless, field research assistants faced some challenges, including the fact that some remote schools were difficult to locate and that roads leading to some schools were in extremely poor condition to the extent that vehicles could not reach those schools. Boda bodas (italics added), which are hired motorcycle taxis, were the only available means to reach some of the remote schools. As a result of poor road conditions and using boda bodas, more time was spent in locating and traveling to each school than the actual time spent in interviewing and collecting data. Furthermore, field research assistants had to make several trips to some schools in order to collect all the data particularly when school administrators were not found at school.

COLLECTING NATIONAL EXAMINATION DATA

The UNEB authorities provided data related to national examinations scores. Once the list of examination centers was obtained and the sample selected, two letters, one of introduction and one of request, were written and sent to the UNEB headquarters in Kyambogo (see Appendix E). The letters contained a brief description of the University, the volunteer program in Uganda, the researchers involved, past research, the intended research, and the rationale for the use of examination scores as a proxy for school performance. A meeting was scheduled to discuss the request with UNEB officials. UNEB officials were accommodating and cooperative. Approval and access was granted basing on several conditions of use. UNEB provided the UCE and UACE examination scores for the 63 secondary schools that had examination centers along with a key to interpret the examination scores. The UCE and UACE scores consisted of the name of the school, the UNEB school code, and the number of candidates that sat for the examinations, and aggregated and subject scores from 2000 up to 2003.

The cost for a computer printout of Mukono District secondary examination scores obtained from UNEB was 100,000 Uganda Shillings, which is approximately US 50 dollars. The computer examination printout included a list of UNEB schools, total number of candidates who sat for the exams, and a summary of aggregated grades obtained by each school.

LIMITATION OF DATA

This study utilized data representing the entire population of UNEB schools, taking into consideration the small number of available UNEB schools in Mukono District. That is, the sample of schools was not random and was limited to description of the population, rather than predictive of a larger population. Irrespective of these sample size and selection related limitations; findings of this study could still be meaningful and useful (Munro, Jacobsen, Duffy, & Braitman, 2001).

Missing data: Some national examination data was not provided for certain schools or could not be read on the data provided. The researcher maintained contacts with UNEB and was finally able to obtain these missing scores. This data was extremely necessary so that our sample did not become even smaller.

Non - response: Two schools declined to participate and two other schools were closed, thus, reducing the number of UNEB schools from the original 67 to 63. This failure of participation these four schools made the sample in this study smaller than was originally planned.

Private candidates: A critical limitation of this study arises from the few schools that allowed private candidates (students from other schools) to sit for UCE examinations from their examination centers. This discrepancy follows that other schools, perhaps for reasons of increasing their revenues through accepting private candidates, might allow lower performing testers to come to their schools. These circumstances seem to suggest the likely real threat in this area is that some prestigious and better performing secondary schools would not allow private candidates. This private candidate scenario might exaggerate the lower performance of certain already lower performing schools, or it might just create larger numbers of exam sitters in schools that are not necessarily consistent with the academic competence of their actual students. This notion of private candidates threatens the validity of the findings and the inferential underpinnings of this study. Given that to identify the actual performance of private candidates from the rest of candidates is extremely difficult in practical sense, since the names of the private candidates were not identified and UCE results generally were aggregated at school level rather than individual student level. The final issue is that we are not really certain what the impact is, but it might be either positive or negative. Consequently, the impact of private candidates might exaggerate the differences in performance across schools, but it remains unclear.

DATA ANALYSIS

Since the data was collected directly from schools, the unit of analysis was the school level, which is the preferred approach when examining school performance (Creemers, 1996; Herpen, 1992; Scheerens, 1991). Data analysis entailed two basic phases. First, the preliminary stage explored the variables and screen for association with school performance. The second stage entailed regression modeling to address the research questions.

Preliminary Data Analysis

The first step in data analysis entailed running a univariate statistics for all the variables in the research model. These statistics included mean, standard deviation (SD), and minimum and maximum values. This preliminary analysis facilitated easy identification of "very extreme or unusual values" (Allison, 1999, p. 78). This preliminary analysis included the school demographic variables.

The second step in the data analysis was to run a Pearson Correlation to screen the variables with the strongest associations with the dependent variable of school performance. With over 600 resource variables available in the archival resource data, this screening process provided the criteria for selecting which variables to represent each type of resource. Correlation was also run between school demographic variables and school performance to identify potentially critical control variables. The full listing of variables screened for association with school performance was presented in Appendix D. The final correlation analysis of the variables included in the model was presented in the findings.

REGRESSION ANALYSIS MODELING

After preliminary data analysis, regression analysis modeled the variables that demonstrated the strongest association with school performance. Regression analysis involved eight regression models. The first model was run with only the control variables. Each of the seven subsequent regression models addressed one of the research hypotheses and included specific variables for that hypothesis as well as the control variables.

The basic regression equation used in this study was:

$$\hat{Y}_{ij} = \alpha + (\beta C)_{ij} + (\beta F)_{ij} + (\beta P)_{ij} + (\beta H)_{ij} + \varepsilon$$

In this formula, the symbols and components represent the following:

1- $\hat{Y}_{ij}$ = the expected school performance score of school i through j expressed as an average value based on standardized national UCE examinations.

2- α = the y-intercept, interpreted as the expected value of UCE scores for a school lacking certain/specific resources.

3- β = the slope term interpreted as change in average UCE scores for each unit increase in any of the resource variables C_{ij} or F_{ij} or P_{ij} or H_{ij} where C = control variables, F = financial related resource variables, P = physical related resource variables, and H = human related resource variables.

4- ε = the error term interpreted as all other factors that affect average UCE scores which are not accounted for in the model.

Thus, the eight regression models will be:

Model 1 – Control variables
Model 2 – Financial resources
Model 3 – Physical resources
Model 4 – Human resources
Model 5 – Financial and physical resources
Model 6 – Physical and human resources
Model 7 – Financial and human resources
Model 8 – All combined resources (financial, physical, and human)

Given that "stepwise regression is the most popular procedure used to obtain the best prediction equation" (Myers & Well, 2003). With stepwise multiple regressions, in sequence independent variables (predictor variables) were added into the regression model to obtain the best predictor variables. Predictor variables that were found to contribute significantly to the model were retained. Conversely, if predictor variables, when added to the model and re-tested no longer contributed significantly to the model, they were removed. That is, predictor variables that generated the least adjusted r-square (R^2) were removed from the model. Nonetheless, a high R^2 does not necessarily mean that the regression model is theoretically important or robust (Miles & Shevlin, 2001). This all suggest is that R^2 should be interpreted cautiously. Sirkin (1995) observed that utilizing R^2 is appropriate to determine the amount of "variations in the dependent variable explained by the dependent variable"(p. 435).

CONCLUSION

This chapter has presented the six research questions that guided this study and the methodology, the conceptual theoretical model, hypotheses, data collection, and data analysis procedures. The constructs in this study were generated from three major categories of resources namely human, financial, and physical. Chapter six presents the findings of this study. It provides tables and figures of descriptive statistics on school and school resources and presents findings obtained from the regression analysis modeling. Chapter seven includes the summary of the study, implications, and conclusions.

CHAPTER SIX

DEMOGRAPHICS AND CONTEXTUAL FACTORS

The primary focus of this study is an exploration of the relationships between various secondary school resource variables on school performance measured by UCE (Uganda Certificate of Education) standardized scores. This chapter is structured to present the findings and results as they relate to each of the six questions and seven hypotheses presented in chapter five. The research questions will function as the super-ordinate categories for this presentation with the hypotheses clustered within each question to which they are related.

Question 1: Demographic and Contextual School Factors

As presented in chapter five, the first question presented in this research project was as follows: What demographic and contextual school factors are critical in secondary school performance? The findings and results relating to this question are presented in the following seven tables which contain descriptive summaries of the demographics and contextual characteristics of schools in Mukono District, Uganda, the sampled area for this study.

Contextual Factors of School Location

Table 6.1 shows the basic contextual factors regarding school location. As can be seen in Table 6.1, most secondary schools are located near the main public transportation routes. That is, 84 percent of the private secondary schools are located within 15 minutes walking distance to main roads, and 78.8 percent of the government-aided secondary schools are similarly situated. In a country with few main roads, and where individuals typically have no personal means of transport (not even personally owned bicycles), this is a remarkable trend.

Chapter 6 - Demographics and Contextual Factors

Table 6.1.
Descriptive Statistics: Basic Contextual Factors of School Location

	Government-aided		Private		Total
Distance from public transport					
Under 5 minute walk distance	7	(37%)	24	(55%)	31
Between 5-15 minute walk distance	8	(42%)	13	(30%)	21
More than 15 minute walk distance	4	(21%)	7	(15%)	11
Total	19		44		63
School on wetlands property					
No wetlands	15	(79%)	27	(61%)	42
Some wetlands	4	(21%)	17	(39%)	35
Total	19		44		63
Is school near homes and shops?					
Few	9	(47%)	24	(55%)	33
Near some	9	(47%)	12	(27%)	21
Near many	1	(6%)	8	(18%)	9
Total	19		44		63

Contextual Factors of Secure Learning Environment

Table 6.2 indicates that creating a safe and secure learning environment for secondary school students is an important aspect of schooling in Mukono District. It can be seen in Table 6.2 that a majority of both government-aided and private secondary schools reported to have lockable front gates and facilities (68.4 per cent and 68.2 percent respectively). Given that a school providing a well-demarcated and secure learning environment is one of the key minimum basic standards for the Ministry of Education (MoES, 2001), it is a bit surprising that only two thirds of the secondary schools have in place that common requirement.

Table 6.2.
Descriptive Statistics: Basic Contextual Factors of Secure Environment

	Government-aided		Private		Total
Front Gate					
Locking	13	(68%)	30	(68%)	43
Gate but not locking	3	(16%)	5	(11%)	8
No gate	3	(16%)	9	(21%)	12
Total	19		44		63

Contextual Factors of School Facilities

Table 6.3 shows the descriptive statistics of the basic contextual factor of school facilities. On land use, 63.6 percent of private secondary schools reported that most of their school land is "useable" compared to 36.8 percent of the government - aided secondary schools. Table 6.3 also shows that 84 percent of the private secondary schools are under construction compared to 63.2 percent of the government - aided schools. Therefore, construction expenses, rather than direct instructional financial outputs are likely consume large portions of the financial budgets of most private secondary schools.

Table 6.3.
Descriptive Statistics: Basic Contextual Factors of School Facilities

	Government – aided		Private		Total
Usability of the land					
Mostly unusable	2	(10%)	1	(02%)	3
Partially unusable	10	(53%)	15	(34%)	25
Mostly usable	7	(37%)	28	(64%)	35
Total	19		44		63
Number of buildings under construction					
0	7	(36%)	7	(16%)	14
1	8	(42%)	30	(68%)	38
2	2	(11%)	6	(14%)	8
3	2	(11%)	None		2
6	None		1	(02%)	1
Total	19		44		63

School Demographics

Table 6.4 shows the characteristics of the secondary schools. Majority of the sampled secondary schools in Mukono District (both government - aided and private) offer both levels of secondary education (UCE and UACE) and are predominantly co - educational (mixed gender) serving both girls and boys.

Table 6.4. *Descriptive Statistics: Secondary School Characteristics*

	Government - aided		Private		Total
School type					
Boarding	2	(10%)	6	(14%)	8
Day	13	(68%)	9	(21%)	22
Combined (boarding & day)	4	(22%)	28	(65%)	32
Total	19		43		62
School level					
A and O levels	13	(68%)	28	(64%)	41
O- levels	6	(32%)	15	(36%)	21
Total	19		43		62
School gender					
Co - educational	17	(90%)	42	(95%)	59
Single gender	2	(10%)	2	(5%)	4
Total	19		44		63

Table 6.5.
Descriptive Statistics: Students Demographics

	Government – aided		Private		Total
Rural students					
0-25 (%)	3	(16%)	7	(16%)	10
26-50 (%)	None		10	(23%)	10
51-75 (%)	2	(10%)	11	(25%)	13
76-100 (%)	14	(74%)	16	(36%)	30
Total	19		44		63
Low income students					
0-25 (%)	1	(5%)	3	(7%)	4
26-50 (%)	2	(11%)	10	(23%)	12
51-75 (%)	3	(16%)	4	(9%)	7
76-100 (%)	13	(68%)	27	(61%)	40
Total	19		44		63

Student Demographics

Table 6.5 shows students' composition in the sampled secondary schools in Mukono District, Uganda. Government - aided secondary schools serve more rural students compared to private secondary schools, and the gap is wide. This finding is not consistent with the recent literature (Bennell & Sayed, 2002b; K. M. Lewin, 2002). These researchers collected their data from four main sources including MoES, NGOs, 13 secondary schools selected from five districts of Uganda.

Question Two: The Status of Secondary School Resources in Mukono Uganda

As presented in chapter five, the second question used in this research project was as follows: What is the current status of resources in secondary schools in Mukono District in Uganda?

The findings and results relating to question two are presented in Tables 6.6, 6.7, 6.8, 6.9, and 6.10. First, the status of financial resources in secondary schools of Mukono Uganda is presented in Table 6.6.

STATUS OF FINANCIAL RESOURCES

Table 6.6 shows the descriptive statistics of school financial resources. Government - aided and private secondary schools differ greatly in quantity and alternative sources of financing. Government -aided schools charge lower fees ranging from 20.000 to 340.000 Uganda Shillings (mean of 100.000 Uganda Shillings) as compared with 30.000 to 389.000 Uganda Shillings (mean of 140.000 Uganda Shillings) charged by private secondary schools.

Government - aided secondary schools, in general, have apparently greater access to grant money than private secondary schools. Table 6.6 indicates that government - aided secondary schools on average receive from the state up to 22.89 million Uganda Shillings in form of Capitation Grants (CG) and 12.95 million Uganda Shillings in the form of Capital Development Funds (CDF). In contrast, private secondary schools do not receive any grant money from the state. Given that CG and CDF are allocated and distributed basing on students' enrollment per school, the more students a school has the higher the amount of capitation grant money received.

Table 6.6.
Descriptive Statistics: Financial in Millions of Uganda Shillings

	Government-aided		Private	
	Mean	SD	Mean	SD
Income resources				
Tuition fees	0.10	0.10	0.14	.09
Revenue per term	68.5	101.4	54.6	76.4
Total revenue 2002	138.5	242.7	90.4	155.5
Fees in-kind	1.2	1.8	6.4	30.2
Government bursary	0.07	0.2	1.2	7.5
Cash donations				
CG	22.9	40.4	...	...
CDF	12.9	55.0	...	...
Church grants	5.3	22.9	.8	4.6
Community funds	1.5	4.8	0.01	0.05
Family contributions			0.3	2.0
NGO grants	26.3	114.7	0.3	1.5
Other (cash)	9.4	22.7	2.1	7.9
Donations in kind	0.6	2.1	1.0	4.7
Financial loans				
Past loans	15.4	57.6	56.6	173.5
Current loans	0.9	3.4	7.2	20.9

Nonetheless, Table 6.6 indicates that private secondary schools seem to rely more on loans than government - aided secondary schools. Private secondary schools received on average up to 56.6 million Uganda Shillings in form of loans compared to the 15.4 million Uganda Shillings received by government - aided secondary schools. As earlier indicated majority of the private secondary schools are under construction, which is reflected by the higher loan averages to meet the extra financing needed to secure building materials and labor costs.

DESCRIPTIVE STATISTICS AND STATUS OF PHYSICAL RESOURCES

In the context of developing countries, many secondary schools virtually lack even the basic school resources such as library, electricity, and separate latrines for girls and boys. Table 6.7 shows the most basic resources that each secondary school ought to have (Nassor & Mohammed, 1998). A striking finding revealed in Table 6.7 is that most secondary schools in Mukono provide these basic school resources such as libraries, electricity, and separate latrines for girls and boys.

Table 6.8 shows the descriptive statistics for physical resources. Overall, the government - aided secondary schools tend to be better off in terms of quality physical resources such as buildings, staff housing and textbooks than private secondary schools. Government - aided secondary schools have twice as many textbooks than private secondary schools. On average government - aided secondary schools check out more textbooks to students and teachers compared to private secondary schools. Further, as may be seen in table 6.8, government - aided secondary schools have relatively greater access to more communication facilities than private secondary schools.

DESCRIPTIVE STATISTICS ON HUMAN RESOURCES

This section presents findings related to human resources in secondary schools of Mukono Uganda. The information provided involves school administrators, teachers and students.

Table 6.7.
Descriptive Statistics: Schools Basic Resources

	Government - aided		Private		Total
Students read in library					
No	10	(53%)	28	(63.6%)	38
Yes	9	(47%)	16	(36.4%)	25
Total	19		44		63
Has electricity					
No	6	(33%)	8	(18.6%)	14
Yes	12	(67%)	35	(81.4%)	47
Total	18		43		61
Does the school have separate pit latrines for boys and girls?					
No	3	(16%)	4	(9.5%)	7
Yes	16	(84%)	38	(90.5%)	54
Total	19		42		61

Table 6.8. *Descriptive Statistics: Physical Resources*

	Government – aided	Private
	Mean	Mean
Instructional materials		
Library textbooks	3276	1646
Books with teachers	155	37
Books with students	592	72
Size of buildings in square feet		
Average total size of buildings	13600	15500
Administration offices	330	320
Classes	1000	1110
Size of land in acres	159	15
	Frequency	Frequency
Facilities		
Has buildings under construction	12 (63 %)	37 (84 %)
Has buildings with glass windows	15 (79 %)	40 (91 %)
Has science laboratory	15 (79 %)	35 (80 %)
Has functioning typewriter	15 (79 %)	34 (77 %)
Has flushing toilets	02 (11 %)	07 (16 %)
Has separate pit latrines for boys & girls	16 (84 %)	42 (91 %)
Facilities		
Has school clinic	08 (42 %)	23 (52 %)
Has entertainment provision	14 (74 %)	34 (77 %)
Staff housing provision	14 (74 %)	24 (55 %)
Communications		
Internet connection	05 (26 %)	02 (4.5 %)
Telephone line	15 (79 %)	31 (71 %)
Functioning fax machine	01 (5.3 %)	02 (4.5 %)
Teachers own m/phones	13 (70 %)	25 (56 %)

Gender of School Administrators

Table 6.9 shows that secondary school administrators are mostly male in Mukono Uganda in both government-aided and private schools. Similarly, most secondary schools have more male than female teachers.

Table 6.9.
Gender of Head Teacher Versus School Ownership

Head teachers' gender	Government - aided		Private		Total
Female	5	(26%)	8	(18%)	13
Male	14	(74%)	36	(82%)	50
Total	19		44		63

Chapter 6 - Demographics and Contextual Factors

Quality of School Administrators

The descriptive statistics show discrepancies exist between government-aided and private secondary schools regarding the quality of school administrators. This is particularly true regarding the education and work experience of administrators.

Education: Table 6.10 shows education qualifications and year of university degree completion for school administrators. Government - aided secondary school administrators tend to be more qualified than their counterparts in private schools. Table 6.10 also indicates that all government - aided secondary school administrators hold, at least, a first university degree compared to 61.4 percent in private schools.

School administrators' experience: Looking at table 6.10 it can be seen that government - aided secondary school administrators on average have three times more working experience than their counterparts in private schools.

Table 6.11 shows the descriptive statistics for additional human resources. Government - aided schools have lower student/ subject teacher ratios in key subjects such as Science, Mathematics, English language and Computer Studies than private secondary schools. Most private secondary schools tend to rely more on part-time teachers for their work force needs in these critical content areas compared to government - aided secondary schools.

Table 6.10.
Level of Education of School Administrators

	Government aided		Private		Total
Type of qualification or university degree					
Diploma in Education	None		10	(23%)	10
BSC/BA	14	(74%)	27	(61%)	41
PGDE	1	(5%)	4	(9%)	5
MA	4	(21%)	3	(7%)	7
Total	19		44		63
University degree completion / qualification dates					
2000-2004	1	(5%)	16	(37%)	17
1995-1999	2	(11%)	23	(57%)	25
1990-1994	5	(26.5%)	2	(4%)	7
1985-1989	2	(11%)	2	(4%)	4
1980-1984	5	(26.5%)			5
1075-1979	2	(11%)			2
1970-1974	1	(5%)	1	(2%)	2
1965-1969	1	(5%)			1
Total	19		44		63

BSC/BA = Bachelor of Science /Bachelor of Arts degree
PGDE = Post Graduate Diploma in Education
MA = Master of Arts

STATUS OF SECONDARY SCHOOL PERFORMANCE IN MUKONO DISTRICT, UGANDA

This section presents the descriptive statistics on secondary school performance in UCE examination scores in Mukono District, Uganda from 2000 to 2003. The descriptive statistics on secondary school performance on standardized UCE scores are summarized in tables 6.12 and 6.13. Secondary school performance of government – aided schools, private schools, and both sectors was combined are compared.

Table 6.11.
Descriptive Statistics: Human Resources

	Government - aided	Private
Average student enrolment		
2001	372	238
2002	438	299
2003	495	378
Average number of teachers per school	27	21
Average student/subject teacher ratio		
Mathematics	139	162
History	114	121
English language	178	187
Biology	185	189
Geography	112	129
Overall student/teacher ratio	18	16
	Frequency	Frequency
Has specialized teachers		
Computer - certified	06 (32 %)	18 (41 %)
Examiners	12 (70.6 %)	25 (58%)
Markers	14 (77.8%)	33 (77 %)
Contracted examiners	04 (25%)	28 (67 %)
Difficult to find	05 (27 %)	09 (22 %)
Status of teachers		
Has teachers who left last year	16 (84 %)	39 (91 %)
Has teachers who live at other schools	12 (63 %)	39 (89 %)
Has teachers who live on campus	04 (27 %)	23 (52 %)
Has administrators who live at school	16 (84 %)	40 (91 %)
Has non - certified teachers	08 (42 %)	16 (37 %)
Has part-time teachers	09 (47%)	27 (61%)

Performance in UCE Examination Scores

Table 6.12 presents the average UCE scores by school type. Findings in table 6.12 suggest that day secondary schools lag behind the rest (boarding and combined) in performance on UCE scores. Note that from 2000 to 2003, the number of UNEB center schools increased by 70 percent from 37 in 2000 to 63 in 2003. Most of the secondary schools that have recently been granted UNEB centers are privately owned.

Care should be taken in reading and understanding the information presented regarding UCE scores. First, in British-style schooling systems such as Uganda the

Chapter 6 - Demographics and Contextual Factors

scale used for grading is virtually the reverse of that used in the United States. For example, in the United States a "grade point average" of 4.0 is typically considered to be the highest level of performance. In the Uganda UCE system, however, a grade of 4.0 is considered the lowest non-failing grade possible. With this in mind the criteria for calculating the average UCE scores is as follows: grade one is multiplied by one, grade two multiplied by two, grade three multiplied by three, grade four is multiplied by four, and fail grade nine is multiplied by five. Then, the accumulated points for each grade product are summed up and divided by the total number of candidates that sat for UCE in each UNEB center school for the year 2003. The smaller the number of average UCE scores the higher the grade. That is, grade one is higher than grade two, and grade two is higher than grade three, and so on.

Figure 6.1 also indicates the performance differences between varying school types. As can be seen some extreme outlying schools exist. Boarding secondary schools did better on average UCE scores than both combined and day schools in all the four years.

This finding suggests that boarding schools may be better than other types of schools in terms of performance on UCE examinations. The debate regarding the pros and cons of boarding secondary schools is beyond the scope of this book.

Table 6.13 shows the yearly average UCE scores of secondary schools by school ownership. As it can be seen from table 6.13, findings suggest that private secondary schools obtained relatively higher average UCE scores for the years 2000, 2001, 2002, and 2003 than government - aided secondary schools.

Table 6.12

Average UCE Scores by School Type

Year	Type	Mean	N	SD
2000	Boarding	1.82	7	0.89
	Day	2.82	16	0.45
	Combined	2.36	14	0.61
2001	Boarding	1.98	7	0.87
	Day	3.02	17	0.51
	Combined	2.65	24	0.60
2002	Boarding	1.98	7	0.87
	Day	3.18	21	0.52
	Combined	2.65	30	0.61
2003	Boarding	1.84	7	0.92
	Day	3.04	21	0.48
	Combined	2.37	30	0.62
Total	Boarding	1.91	28	0.84
	Day	3.03	75	0.49
	Combined	2.53	98	0.62

The mean differences between boarding and day are significant at the 0.05 level. N.B. The smaller the mean value the higher the grade.

School Resources and Performance in Developing Countries

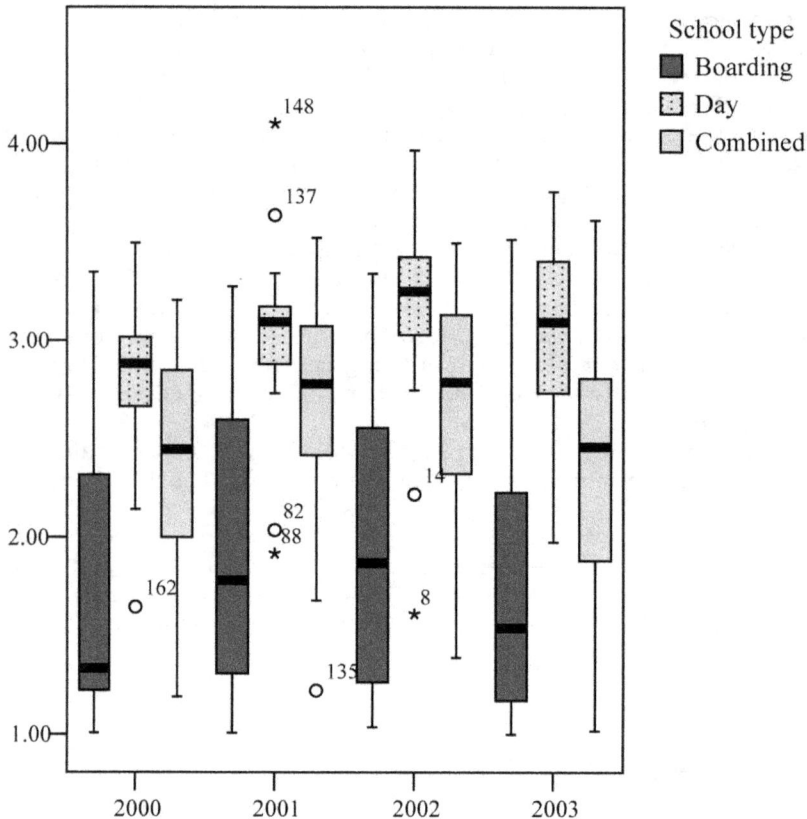

Figure 6.1. Average UCE Scores by School Type

Figure 6.2 Shows Average Yearly UCE Scores by School Ownership. This finding is poignant because, first of all, the best performing (statistical "outliers") schools are mostly government - aided secondary schools. Secondly, most private secondary schools are newer, smaller, and less endowed with rudimentary educational resources than government - aided secondary schools.

Further, Figure 6.2 also informatively presents the distribution of school performance data on UCE. Based on the work of Miles and Shevlin (2001), the researcher used Boxplot to examine whether the distribution of UCE school performance data deviated substantially from normality. As can be seen in figure 6.1, a few government-aided and private secondary schools are extreme outliers in their performance in UCE examination scores.

Another exciting finding is revealed when comparing the 50th percentile (median) in figure 6.2. Private secondary schools seem to show higher performance compared to government - aided secondary schools.

Table 6.13
Average UCE Scores of Secondary Schools by School Ownership and Year of Examination

Year	Ownership	Mean	N	SD
2000	Government-aided	2.56	18	0.66
	Private	2.37	19	0.74
2001	Government-aided	2.76	19	0.72
	Private	2.63	29	0.68
2002	Government-aided	2.88	19	0.74
	Private	2.73	40	0.71
2003	Government-aided	2.76	19	0.79
	Private	2.47	40	0.69
Total	Government-aided	2.74	75	0.73
	Private	2.57	128	0.71

The mean differences btween government-aided and private are not significant at 0.05 level. Note that, the smaller the mean value the higher the grade.

Prior Academic Students' Achievement

Many researchers have recommended the need to know the prior academic students' achievement in projecting the relationships between school resources and school performance (Scheerens, 2001b). Table 6.14 presents prior academic students' achievement at senior one level. In terms of prior academic students' achievement, as revealed by findings and results in table 6.14, government - aided secondary schools on average tend to enroll students who perform slightly lower academic levels than private secondary schools, but the mean differences are not statistically significant based on ANOVA.

Results for Research Questions 3, 4, 5 and 6

As presented in chapters five research questions 3, 4, 5, and 6 in this study were as follows:

Research Question 3: What is the relationship between financial resources and performance in secondary schools in Mukono District, in Uganda?

Research Question 4: What is the relationship between physical resources and performance in secondary schools in Mukono District, in Uganda?

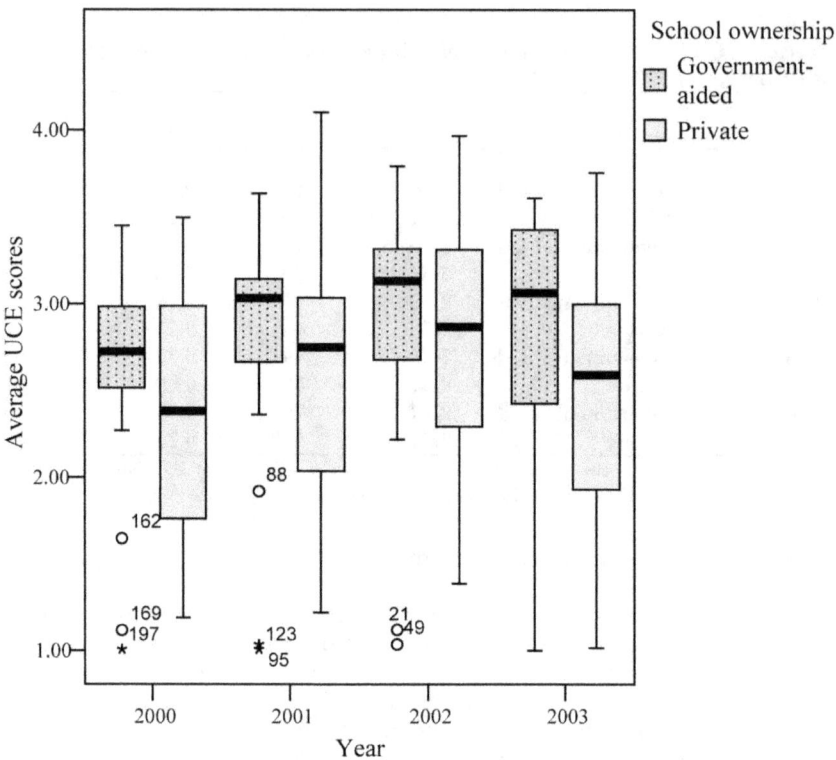

Figure 6.2 Average UCE Scores by School Ownership and Year

Table 6.14
Descriptive Statistics and ANOVA: Prior Students Achievement by School Ownership

Type	N	Mean	SD	SE	Minimum	Maximum
Government – aided	17	17.74	7.10	1.72	5	31
Private	36	17.12	4.23	0.71	8	27
Total	53	17.32	5.26	0.72	5	31

	Sum of squares	df	ANOVA Mean Square	F	Sig.
Between groups	4.399	1	4.399	.156	.694
Within groups	1435.495	51	28.147		
Total	1439.894	52			

Research Question 5: What is the relationship between human resources and performance in secondary schools in Mukono District, in Uganda?

Chapter 6 - Demographics and Contextual Factors

Research Question 6: How are all types of resources (financial, physical, and human) related to performance in secondary schools in Mukono District, in Uganda?

The findings and results of research questions 3 through 6 will be presented in two phases namely: First, results of the descriptive statistics and correlation analysis are presented in table 6.15 followed by the findings and results of regression modeling analysis presented in subsequent tables 6.16 through 6.24.

CORRELATIONAL RELATIONSHIPS BETWEEN VARIABLES ON SCHOOL PERFORMANCE

The correlational findings and results for these four research questions are presented in this section. Table 6.15 presents descriptive statistics and correlations of control variables (effect of school levels, percentage of low-income students, and standardized[5] prior academic students' achievement), and various resource (financial, physical, and human) variables on school performance. Only important correlations (in terms effect size) with the dependent variable are presented in the correlation matrix. It is important to note that the smaller the average UCE score the higher is the grade. Thus, the negative and positive correlations of independent variables with the dependent variable (average UCE scores) can be interpreted as follows: negative correlation means that lowering the independent variable can be associated with increase in the average UCE scores, which actually implies a lower grade. The reverse is true for positive correlations of the independent variable with the dependent variable. Findings show that school performance (dependent variable) showed high positive correlation with the percentage of low-income students, indicating that secondary schools serving higher percentages low-income students tend to perform worse in UCE examination scores. This finding is consistent with the current literature. Glassed buildings seem to be correlated with school revenue and are statistically significant. Interestingly, findings in table 6.15 also show that the part - time teacher variable is negatively related to the teachers with mobile phones variable and is statistically significant. This finding seems to suggest that part - time teachers are less likely to own mobile phone.

Table 6.15

Descriptive Statistics and Correlations of Control and Resource Variables

		N	Mean	SD	1	2	3	4	5	6	7	8	9
1	UCE Scores	59	2.57	.74	1								
2	% of Low-income student	63	3.32	.99	.569***								
3	Prior students' achievement	53	22.68	5.26	-.508***	-.306*							
4	School revenue	61	5.24	5.05	-.679***	-.561***	.436***						
5	Past loans	62	43.95	148	-.431***	-.436***	.308*	.299*					
6	Library use	63	.40	.49	-.504***	-.391***	.367***	.568***	.293*				
7	Flushing toilets	63	.14	.35	-.422**	-.314**	.334**	.453***	.048	.132			
8	Internet connection	63	.11	.32	-.380***	-.113	.239	.530***	.276*	.229	.258*		
9	Science laboratory	63	1.13	1.27	-.517***	-.44***	.500***	.584***	.483***	.482***	.378***	.353***	
10	Glassed building	63	.51	.34	-.488***	-.511***	.365***	.537***	.171	.307**	.338***	.437***	.214
11	Electricity	61	.77	.44	-.430***	-.268*	.218	.274*	.166	.296*	.243*	.227	.074
12	Student' computers	62	.37	.48	-.540***	-.472***	.381***	.651***	.185	.458***	.501***	.537***	.254*
13	Entertainment		.90	.65	-.194	.023	.211	.034	.186	-.083	.148	.061	.053
14	Teachers' phones %	62	.53	.51	-.401***	-.527***	.378***	.489***	.290*	.431***	.348***	.227	.323**
15	Examiners %	59	.11	.16	-.212	-.281*	.300*	.312***	.092	.129	.187	.317**	.222
16	Markers %	60	.09	.17	-.177	-.331**	.007	.013	.010	.122	.020	-.002	-.189
17	Teacher/student ratio	62	16.60	6.07	-.210	-.344***	.293*	.336***	.329**	.303**	.190	.438***	.246*
18	Part-time teachers %	61	.21	.24	.042	.036	.049	-.211	.111	.023	-.077	-.010	-.075
19	Female teachers %	63	.23	.16	-.338***	-.341***	.254	.229	.541***	.357***	.197	.003	.131
20	Teacher hard to get	60	5.65	6.46	-.305*	-.179	.299*	.529***	.190	.267*	.242	.285*	.579***
21	Examiner contract %	60	.13	.25	-.292*	-.400**	.364***	.312***	.371***	.200	.216	.164	.108
22	Math teachers %	63	3.06	2.11	-.585***	-.341***	.376***	.732***	.340***	.454***	.363***	.355***	.639***
23	History teachers %	63	3.89	2.08	-.376***	-.502***	.316*	.558***	.177	.357***	.221	.285*	.482***
24	English teachers %	63	2.3	1.43	-.623***	-.387***	.489***	.689***	.310**	.480***	.338***	.451***	.560***
25	Biology teachers %	63	2.4	1.60	-.465***	-.336***	.356**	.616***	.290*	.300**	.244*	.236	.671***
26	Chemistry teachers %	63	2.6	1.99	-.489***	-.383***	.356***	.620***	.284	.314**	.222	.391***	.668***
27	Geography teachers %	63	3.8	1.90	-.193	-.140	.233	.316**	.155	.041	.074	.158	.380***

Table 6.15 (Continued)

		10	11	12	13	14	15	16	17	18	19	20
8	Internet connection											
9	Science laboratory											
10	Glassed building	.440***	1									
11	Electricity	.132	0407***									
12	Student' computers	.360***	.525***	.435***								
13	Entertainment	.114	-.143	-.083	-.075							
14	Teachers' phones %	.359***	.309**	.176	.224	-.023						
15	Examiners %	.538***	.227	.082	.191	.175	.410***					
16	Markers %	.055	.399***	-.081	.104	-.203	-.055	-.013				
17	Teacher/student ratio	.246*	.369***	.188	.308**	-.101	.462***	.249*	.060			
18	Part-time teachers %	-.026	-.026	.145	-.048	.094	-.255*	-.232	-.143	-.038		
19	Female teachers %	.298**	.157	.224	.159	.098	.283	.035	-.004	.271	.357	
20	Teacher hard to get	.470***	.250*	.112	.232	.096	.256*	.320	-.186	.237	.043	.236
21	Examiner contract %	.413***	.116	.106	.247*	.132	.423***	1	-.013	.249*	-.241	.446
22	Math teachers %	.749***	.397***	.147	.410***	.135	.433***	.411***	-.206	.211	-.016	.170
23	History teachers %	.405***	.443***	.170	.324**	.076	.405***	.298*	.083	.268*	-.022	.008
24	English teachers %	.577***	.426***	.288*	.419***	.174	.562***	.326***	-.248	.354***	-.119	.263
25	Biology teachers %	.494***	.294**	.223	.320**	.196	.488***	.290*	-.221	.318**	.011	.182
26	Chemistry teachers %	.607***	.365***	.167	.319**	.270*	.431***	.442***	-.186	.402***	.032	.140
27	Geography teachers %	.314**	.148	.086	.170	.118	.249*	.478***	-.118	.206	-.213	-.005

*** Correlation is significant at the 0.001 level (2-tailed), ** Correlation is significant at the 0.01 level (2-tailed), * Correlation is significant at the 0.05 level (2-tailed)

Table 6.15 (Continued)

		21	22	23	24	25
23	History teachers %	.589***				
24	English teachers %	.774***	.497***			
25	Biology teachers %	.696***	.626***	.629***		
26	Chemistry teachers %	.788***	.683***	.700***	.817***	
27	Geography teachers %	.503***	.583***	.357***	.505***	.536***

*** Correlation is significant at the 0.001 level (2-tailed), ** Correlation is significant at the 0.01 level (2-tailed), * Correlation is significant at the 0.05 level (2-tailed)

REGRESSION MODELING RESULTS

In the following section research questions 3, 4, 5, and 6 superimposed by the seven hypotheses are addressed below. The findings and results for each of the eight regression models are presented in tables 6.16 through 6.24. In each case, the researcher reports the standardized coefficient (beta), standard error (SE), and regression statistics including coefficient of multiple determination (R^2), change in R^2, F-value, and significance p-values.

Additional research question: Relationship Between Control Variables and School Performance

Given that all the three control variables (school levels, percentage of low-income students, and prior students' achievement) were included in all the eight regression models, then, it was prudent to run an independent model for only control variables and school performance. Therefore, the regression model 1 examined the relationship between the control variables and school performance. Table 6.16 presents the regression model 1 results. Findings indicate statistical significant relationships between the control variables and school performance.

Model 1 accounts for 45.3 per cent (that is adjusted R^2 .453) in the variation of UCE exam scores (dependent variable). The regression coefficient for the percentage of low-income students is positive and has strong statistical significance on school performance. Similarly, the regression coefficient prior students' achievement is positive and has strong statistical significance with school performance. This finding is consistent with the literature and therefore all the three control variables were included in all subsequent regression models. Findings and results of model 1 provided a platform for comparing the relative strengths of different types of resource variables in subsequent regression models.

Table 6.16
Model 1: Control Variable and School Performance

	Variables	Beta (β)	SE
Control variables	% of low-income students	.379***	.095
	School level	-.272***	.100
	Prior students' achievement	.327***	.016

	R^2	Adjusted R^2	ΔR^2	F	p	df
Regression statistics	.487	.453	...	14.257	.000	3, 45

*** Coefficient is significant at the $p \leq 0.001$ level, *Coefficient is significant at the $p \leq 0.05$ level

Results for Research Question 3: Financial Resources and School Performance

The third research question presented in chapter five states: What is the relationship between financial resources and performance in secondary schools in Mukono District, in Uganda?

Hypothesis 1: Secondary schools in in Mukono District, in Uganda with more financial resources will perform higher on examination scores than other schools.

Regression results for model 2 appear in table 6.17. Findings indicate strong positive statistical significant relationships between square root of total school revenue and school performance on standardized UCE examinations scores, thus supporting hypothesis I. Controlling for school level, prior students' achievement, and percentage of low-income students, model 2 accounted for only 4.8 per cent (that is adjusted $R^2 = .535$, $p \leq .000$) in the variation of school performance on UCE scores (dependent variable).

Interestingly, financial resource variables seem to account for an extremely small influence on UCE school performance. The relationship between financial resources on school performance is too weak to accept with confidence the validity and correctness of hypothesis I.

Results for Research Question 4: Physical Resources and School Performance

The fourth research question presented in chapter five states: What is the relationship between physical resources and performance in secondary schools in Mukono District, in Uganda?
Hypothesis 2: Secondary schools in Mukono District, in Uganda with more physical resources will perform higher in examination scores than other schools.

Table 6.17
Model 2: Financial Resource Variables on School Performance

	Variables	Beta (β)	SE
Control variables	% of low-income students	.188*	.107
	School level	-.175	.202
	Prior students' achievement	-.097	.017
Financial resource	Square root of school revenues	-.423***	.015
	Filling revenue reports	-.175*	.076
	Value of past loans	Ex	
	Government support	Ex	
	Extent of government t support	Ex	

Regression statistics	R^2	Adjusted R^2	ΔR^2	F	p	df
	.585	.535	.048	11.574	.000	5, 41

*** Coefficient is significant at the $p \leq 0.001$ level, *Coefficient is significant at the $p \leq 0.05$ level, Ex = excluded from the model

Table 6.18 shows findings and results of regression model 3 for research question 4 examining the relationship between physical resources variables and school performance. Findings in table 6.18 indicate negative statistically significant relationships between some physical resource variables and school performance on UCE standardized exams scores.

Controlling for school level, students' prior achievement, and percentage of low-income students—model 3 on physical resource variables accounted for 16.1 per cent (that is adjusted $R^2 = .648$, p (.000) in the variation of school performance on UCE scores. Thus these findings and results support hypothesis II of this study.

Chapter 6 - Demographics and Contextual Factors

Results of Research Question 5: Human Resources and School Performance

The fifth research question presented in chapter five states: What is the relationship between human resources and performance in secondary schools in Mukono District, in Uganda?
Hypothesis 3: Secondary schools in Mukono District, in Uganda with more human resources will perform higher in examination scores than other schools.
Table 6.19 shows findings and results of regression model 4 for research question 5 examining the relationship between human resources and school performance.

Table 6.18
Model 3: Physical Resource Variables on School Performance

	Variables	Beta (β)	SE
Control variables	% of low -income students	.291**	.109
	School level	-.162	.177
	Prior students' achievement	-.072	.015
Physical resource	Library use	-.215*	.160
	Book-student ratio	-.124*	.007
	Flushing toilet provision	-.229**	.234
	Internet connection	-.101*	.226
	Science laboratory	Ex	
	Building with glasses	Ex	
	Electricity	-.184*	.177
	Entertainment provision	-.090	.124
Regression statistics	R^2 Adjusted R^2 (R2 F p df		
	.708 .648 .161 11.814 .000 9, 38		

*** Coefficient is significant at the p (0.001 level, ** Coefficient is significant at the p (0.01 level,
*Coefficient is significant at the p (0.05 level, Ex = excluded from the model

The findings and results in table 6.19 indicate negative statistical significant relationships between some human resource variables and school performance on standardized UCE examinations scores. These findings and results, thus, support hypothesis III. Furthermore, controlling for school level, prior students' achievement, and percentage of low-income students—results show that human resources accounted/explained for only 10.8 per cent (that is adjusted R2 = .595, p (.000) in the variation of school performance on UCE scores.

Results of Research Question 6: Effects of Different Resource Combinations on School Performance

Research question 6 as presented in chapter five states: How is the combination of all three types of resources (financial, physical, and human) related to performance in secondary schools in Mukono District, in Uganda? Research question 6 is examined basing on four hypotheses from hypotheses 4 through 8. Each of these four hypotheses is examined in an independent regression model (that is models 5 through 8). Findings and results obtained from these regression models

5 through 8 are presented in tables 6.20, 6.21, 6.22, and 6.23 respectively.

Table 6.19
Model 4: Human Resource Variables on School Performance

	Variables	Beta (β)	SE
Control variables	% of low-income students	.233*	.119
	School level	-.074	.182
	Prior students' achievement	.008	.017
Human resource	Examiners %	Ex	
	Markers contracted %	Ex	
	Student-teacher ratio	-.106	.090
	Female teacher %	-.177	.135
	Part-time teacher %	Ex	
	Boarding student %	-.188*	.200
	English teacher %	-.455***	.073
Regression statistics	R^2 = .639	Adjusted R^2 = .595	(R2 .108) F = 14.494 p = .000 df = 7, 40

*** Coefficient is significant at the level p (0.001, ** Coefficient is significant at the level p (0.01,
*Coefficient is significant at the level p (0.05, Ex = excluded from the model

Hypothesis 4: Secondary schools in Mukono District, in Uganda with more of financial and physical resources will perform higher in examination scores than other schools.

Table 6.20 indicates results of regression model 5 for research question 6, examining the effect of combining financial and physical resources variables on school performance. The results in table 6.20 also show strong negative statistical significant relationships on school performance. Furthermore, controlling for school level, prior students' achievement, and percentage of low-income students—this regression model 5 (comprising financial and physical resources variables) accounted for 16.3 per cent (that is adjusted R2 = .650, p (.000) in the variation on school performance on UCE scores. These results support the fourth hypothesis of this study.

Hypothesis 5: Secondary schools in Mukono District, in Uganda with more of physical and human resources combined will perform higher in examination scores than other schools.

Chapter 6 - Demographics and Contextual Factors

Table 6.20
Model 5: Combined Financial and Physical Resource Variables on School Performance

	Variables	Beta (β)	SE
Control variables	% of low-income students	.241*	.004
	School level	.107	.173
	Prior students' achievement	.047	.016
Financial resource	Square root of school revenue	-.182	.024
	Filing revenue report	-.132	.167
Physical resource	Library use	Ex	
	Book-student ratio	-.234**	.007
	Flushing toilet provision	-.317***	.236
	Internet connection	Ex	
	Electricity	-.208*	.166
	Entertainment provision	.111	.118
Regression statistics	R^2 .734	Adjusted R^2 .650	ΔR^2 .163	F 9.525	p .000	df 9, 31

*** Coefficient is significant at the p (0.001 level, ** Coefficient is significant at the p (0.01 level, *Coefficient is significant at the p (0.05 level, Ex = excluded from the model

Table 6.21 shows results of regression model 6 for research question 6 to determine the relative effect of each resource variable (physical and human) on school performance.

Table 6.21
Model 6: Physical and Human Resource Variables on School Performance

	Variables	Beta (β)	SE
Control variables	% of low-income students	.271**	.086
	School level	-.093	.180
	Prior students' achievement	.083	.016
Physical resources	Library use	Ex	
	Flushing toilet provision	-.194*	.237
	Internet connection	Ex	
	Electricity	-.185*	.185
	Entertainment provision	-.083	.112
Human resource	Markers contracted %	Ex	
	English teacher %	-.392**	.081
	Boarding student %	-.322***	.228
	Teacher/student ratio	.076	.013
Regression statistics	R^2 .700	Adjusted R^2 .639	ΔR^2 .152	F 11.382	p .000	df 9, 34

*** Coefficient is significant at the p $\leq$0.001 level, ** Coefficient is significant at the p $\leq$0.01 level
*Coefficient is significant at the p (0.05 level, Ex = excluded from the model

Controlling percentage of low-income students, school level, and prior students' achievement results of regression model 6 revealed that a combination of physical and human resources accounted for 15.2 per cent (that is adjusted R2 = 639, p ≤ .000) in the variation of school performance on UCE scores. Findings in table 6.21 also show that percentage of the English teacher variable seems to be the highest predictor on school performance.

Hypothesis 6: Secondary schools in Mukono District, in Uganda with more of financial and human resources will perform higher in examination scores than other schools.

Table 6.22 shows the findings and results of regression Model 7 for research question 6 to determine the relative effect of each type of resource variable (financial, and human) on school performance. Findings in table 6.22 revealed that regression model 7 accounts for 13.4 per cent (that isi.e. adjusted R2 =621, p (.000) in the variation on school performance. Even in this model, the percentage of English teacher variable seems to be the strongest predictor and has a negative strong statistical significant relationship on school performance.

Table 6.22
Model 7: Financial and Human Resource Variables on School Performance

	Variables	Beta	SE
Control variables	% of low-income students	.349**	.117
	School level	-.022	.191
	Prior students' achievement	.010	.017
Financial resources	Square root of school revenues	-.039	.029
	Filing revenue reports	-.230*	.168
	Past loans	Ex	
Human resource	Examiners %	Ex	
	Markers contracted %	Ex	
	Student-teacher ratio	.114	.014
	Boarding students %	-.109	.254
	English teacher %	-.487***	.078
Regression statistics	R^2 Adjusted R^2 ΔR^2 F p df		
	.690 .621 .134 10.024 .000 8, 36		

*** Coefficient is significant at the p ≤0.001 level, ** Coefficient is significant at the p ≤0.01 level,
*Coefficient is significant at the p ≤0.05 level, Ex = excluded from the model

Hypothesis 7: Secondary schools in Mukono District, in Uganda with more of all types of resources (financial, physical, and human) will perform highest in examination scores than other schools.
Table 6.23 shows the results of regression model 8 for research question 6 to determine the strength of the effect of each of the three resource types (financial, physical, and human) on school performance. Findings presented in Table 6.23 indicated that regression model 8 accounted for 22 per cent (that is adjusted R2 = 707, p ≤ .000) in the variation of school performance on UCE scores. This finding supports hypothesis 7 of this study. Interestingly, at least, each of the three main

Chapter 6 - Demographics and Contextual Factors

types of resources (human, financial, and physical) contributed in final regression model 8, but with different effect sizes.

Furthermore, the filing revenue reports variable has a negative statistical significant relationship on school performance. This implies that secondary schools in Mukono District, in Uganda that file revenue reports tend to perform better in UCE examination scores than others. Finally, table 6.24 presents the overall summary of findings and results from all the eight regression models. As can be seen in table 6.24, findings show that the percentage of low-income students' variable has a positive statistically significant relationship on school performance in seven out of the eight regression models (7/8) analyzed in this study.

Table 6.23
Model 8: Financial, Physical, and Human Resource Variables on School Performance

	Variables	Beta	SE
Control variables	% of low-income students	.151	.005
	School level	.072	.165
	Prior students' achievement	-.028	.016
Financial resources	Square root of school revenue	-.099	.029
	Filling revenue reports	-.159**	.149
Physical resources	Library use		
	Flushing toilet provision	-.212**	.219
	Internet connection	Ex	
	Electricity	-.204**	.160
	Entertainment provision	-.079	.117
Human resources	Markers contracted %	Ex	
	English teacher %	-.385***	.068
	Boarding student %	-.249**	.243
	Student-teacher ratio	.145	.014

Regression statistics	R^2	Adjusted R^2	ΔR^2	F	p	df
	.782	.707	.220	10.445	.000	11,32

*** Coefficient is significant at the $p \leq 0.001$ level, ** Coefficient is significant at the $p \leq 0.01$ level,
*Coefficient is significant at the $p \leq 0.05$ level, Ex = excluded from the model

Further striking results in table 6.24 include the three resource variables--flushing toilets, electricity, and percentage of English teachers—that each of them have negative statistical significant relationships on school performance in four out of four (4/4) regression models in which these resource variables were entered.

Table 6.24
Overall Summary Stepwise Regression Results

Model	(1)	(2)	(3)	(4)	(5)	(6)	(7)	(8)
Control Variables								
% of Low-income students	.379***	.188*	.291***	.233*	.241*	.271**	.349**	.151
School level	-.272***	-.175	-.162	-.074	.107	-.093	-.022	.072
Prior students' achievement	.327***	-.097	-.072	.008	.047	-.083	.010	-.028
Financial Resources								
Sq.rt. of school revenue		-.423***			-.182		-.039	-.099
Filing revenue reports		-.176*			-.132		-.230*	-.159*
Physical Resources								
Library use			-.215*		Ex			Ex
Book/student ratio			-.124*		-.234**			
Flushing toilets			-.229*		-.317***	-.194*		-.212**
Internet connection			-.101*		Ex	Ex		Ex
Electricity			-.184*		-.208*	-.185*		-.204**
Entertainment provision			-.090		-.111	-.083		-.079
Human Resources								
Teacher/student ratio				-.106		.076	.114	.145
Female teachers				-.177		Ex		
Boarding students %				-.188*		-.322**	-.109	-.249**
English teachers %				-.455***		-.392**	-.487***	-.385***
Adjusted R^2 (effect size)	.453	.535	.648	.595	.650	.639	.621	.707
ΔR^2 (compared to model 1)	...	.048	.161	.108	.163	.152	.134	.220
F	14.257	11.574	11.814	14.494	9.525	11.382	10.024	9.316
df (regression, residual)	3, 45	5, 41	9, 38	7, 40	9, 31	9, 34	8, 36	11, 32

*p ≤0.05, **p ≤0.01, ***p ≤0.001, Ex = excluded from the model

It is important to note that the results of collinearity diagnostics conducted revealed no multicollinearity problems in any of the eight regression models. The tolerance statistics generated in the regression models were greater than 0.5 which indicates low probability of multicollinearity (Allison, 1999; Munro, 2001b).

CONCLUSION

This chapter covered empirical findings and results generated to examine six research questions and superimposed by seven hypotheses. The methodological techniques adopted included, descriptive statistics to investigate the first two research questions. Inferential statistics generated using correlation - regression analysis techniques addressed the last four research questions in this study. This study has revealed that huge discrepancies exist, in terms of resource endowment between government - aided and private secondary schools. This study has also showed that a few secondary schools maintained and sustained their performance on UCE scores over the four year period (2000-2003). Overall, findings of this study suggested that secondary schools with more of all the resources (financial, human, and physical) tended to outperform others. The following chapter presents a summary, implications and conclusions of this study.

CHAPTER SEVEN

THEORETICAL AND PRACTICAL IMPLICATIONS OF RBV SUMMARY, IMPLICATIONS AND CONCLUSIONS

This chapter is divided into three sections presenting a summary of the study, theoretical and policy implications, and general conclusions. The importance of using the RBV (resource-based view) and VRISE (valuable, rare, inimitable, non-substitutable, and exploitable) interpretive framework are central to each of these sections. Aside from the issues arising from the data, in a very real sense the indispensability of having and using a theoretical and interpretive framework emerged as one of, if not the most salient, finding of this study.

> The effect of resources depends on both access and use: students and teachers cannot use resources they do not have, but the resources they do have are not self-acting. Simply collecting a stock of conventional resources cannot create educational quality, for quality does not arise simply from these attributes (Cohen, et al., 2003, p. 122).

As Cohen and his colleagues point out, the notion of educational resources and their impact on school performance and educational quality remains obscure and highly contested. The notion of educational resources and school performance becomes even further confounded in situations of abysmal poverty common in developing countries.

Nevertheless, in the pursuit of educational quality, numerous resources have been highlighted in the research and narrative literature as being related to school performance outcomes, but those that best contribute to school performance and why they do so is not clearly and consistently spelled out. The primary purpose of this study was to explore the relationships between resources and school performance as measured by standardized UCE exams scores in secondary schools in Mukono District, in Uganda More specifically; the study analyzed salient financial, physical, and human resources variables using correlational methods. Descriptive and inferential statistics were generated and presented in chapter four. The following section presents and discusses only the most salient findings drawn from the research questions of this study.

RESULTS BASED ON THE RESEARCH QUESTIONS

Research questions 1 and 2 explored the descriptive and contextual factors of school resources in secondary schools in Mukono District, in Uganda. The results of that exploration revealed huge disparities in terms of resource endowments between government - aided and private secondary schools. In general, government - aided secondary schools were more resource advantaged than private schools.

While all seven hypotheses were supported by the findings and results presented in this study, the size of effect differed widely. Reviewing the overall pattern of significant resource variables across all the regression models in table 6.24, it can be seen that physical resources have the highest number of significant results (12 of 32), followed by control variables with 9 of 32, human resources with 7 of 32, and finally financial resources with 4 of 32.

Correspondingly, in the separate analytical models, financial resources accounted for the least (4.8 per cent) in the variation of school performance on UCE examinations whereas the physical resources accounted for the highest (16.1 per cent) in the variation of school performance on UCE examinations. On the other hand, when physical resources and human resources were combined in regression model 6, they only accounted for 15.2 per cent in the variation of school performance on UCE examinations. This decrease in ability to explain the variation in the school performance when the physical resource and financial resource variables were entered in a combined model is likely due to the smaller number of complete records that could be included in the more complex analysis of two versus one kind of resource. This analytical challenge is not unusual, but should indicate caution when comparing the results of simple analyses compared to those with more complex combinations of different variables.

REGRESSION MODEL 8 RESULTS

The most complex combination of variables was found in regression model 8, which addressed research question six and hypothesis seven. As can be seen in table 6.24, while all three control variables (that is percentage of low-income students, school level and prior student achievement) were found to be positively related to school performance, none of them was statistically significant in this regression model. The most exciting finding is that the effect of all control variables seems to be lowest in the final combined regression model 8, at least based on the beta values. Yet, all control variables presented strong statistical significant relationships with the criterion variable in a separate regression model 1.

The lack of statistically significant relationship for all control variables in the more complex regression model suggests the possibility, perhaps even likelihood, that student/family characteristics and prior student achievement in the "simpler" regression models acted as "proxy" measures for some of the predictor variables included in the more complex regression model 8. For instance, a high percentage of low income students may be a proxy measure for the condition that a school attracting these types of students will be less likely to have more access to all the three kinds of important resources (financial, physical, and human). Further, in the more complex model 8 these potentially "proxied" conditions are specifically accounted for, thus reducing the manifest impact of the earlier significant variables in the more simple models. The reverse may be true for a school enrolling a high percentage of high income students.

Recognizing this dilemma, it is important to note that the final regression model accounted for the highest amount of variation (22 percent) in school performance, compared to all other seven models in this study. Further, the effect size of the adjusted R2 is 70.7 per cent, again the highest in all of the models.

Although almost 30 per cent of the variation in school performance remains unexplained and might require further empirical inquiry, an adjusted R2 of 70.7 percent is a robust figure, and should be of great interest and use to policy makers. Furthermore, reviewing the final regression model (table 6.24), each of the three main types of resources (financial, physical, and human) has one or two elements that were statistically significant in school performance in the final model. This finding indicates that each of the three types of resources are complementary, and contribute much more to the variation on school performance than they do when considered separately.

The most poignant finding (in terms of statistical significance) was that human resources turned out to be the most influential resource variable in the final model. The "percentage of English teacher" variable proved to be the best predictor of school performance, and represented a strong statistically significant relationship (β = -.385; p ≤ .0001). This finding is intuitively reasonable because English is the official medium of communication and instruction in Ugandan secondary schools, albeit not the typical "native language" or "home language" of most of the students. Therefore, it is quite reasonable to believe that secondary schools with more trained English language teachers could perform better on UCE examinations than the others, since students with a better command of English would tend to understand the curriculum content and subject matter with more ease than other students leading to better performance in English language based UCE examinations.

Another exciting finding is that filing revenue reports is associated with higher performance in UCE examinations in schools in Mukono District, in Uganda. Whether filing revenue reports is a proxy for more important factors such better management of school resources and accountability was not investigated by this study and remains unanswered. However, filing revenue reports can also be associated with effective and efficient use of financial and material resources—thus, freeing some additional resources that could be utilized to implement other important educational programs to improve school performance. We now turn to the question raised by these findings and the results already presented in chapter six: What do we learn from the findings as filtered by the RBV?

THEORETICAL AND POLICY IMPLICATIONS

By using the RBV as an interpretive lens, this study offers an alternative to the production function model as a way of looking at school resources and school performance. The RBV perspective is, therefore, central in the theoretical and practical interpretation of the findings and results in this study. This study also advances the literature by attempting to show the rationale for how and why the RBV could extend knowledge beyond the production function model.

THEORETICAL IMPLICATIONS OF USING RBV/VRISE

According to the RBV, the theoretical working assumption of this study was that secondary schools with more of the resources akin to Barney's VRISE attributes would tend to enjoy superior performance (Barney, 1991a). Given that secondary schools consistently continue to maintain resources that vary in Barney's VRISE attributes (resource heterogeneity), then, systematic differences in performance across these secondary schools would theoretically exist. Further, these differences among secondary schools may be quite stable (resource immobility) for long periods (Foss, 2000). It is not surprising that secondary schools in the sample of this study tended to maintain their superior performance positions on UCE examinations over the four-year period (2000-2003). Indeed, Foss (2000) asserted that the way organizations control the key critical resources could lead to organizational performance differences. In practical sense, one could speculate that a school that files revenue reports and maintains proper records of its resources is more likely to outperform others on UCE scores. This speculation suggests a need to study both the context in which resources are used, as well as how they are used, to be able to understand better the relationships between resources and school performance. Based on this study, what really matters is to possess advantage creating resources and to have the ability to use them over long periods.

However, advantage creating resources may continue to lead to superior performance so long as fewer schools have easy access to them. The moment many schools get access to a previously unique advantage creating resource, then the advantage enjoyed by a few schools that used to control and monopolize that particular resource has the potential to be eroded within a very short time (Koruna & Luggen, 2003). Given this perspective, schools would be expected to avoid helping direct "competitors" from gaining easy access to their critical advantage creating resources. Under normal circumstances, schools must safeguard and protect their critical advantage creating resources from their market competitors. Keeping other factors equal, those schools that succeed to acquire, maintain, and protect their advantage creating resources from their competitors would, therefore, tend to enjoy sustainable superior performance for long periods.

PRACTICAL IMPLICATIONS OF RBV

What do these findings and results of the regression models mean in terms of practical implications of using the RBV as the interpretive framework for this set of data and analyses? Out of the 20 total variables included in the regression models, the discussion and interpretation will only focus on a few most salient variables. The rationale for selecting the resource variables included in the final theoretical discussion and interpretation was based on either one or both of the following conditions: 1 a resource should be high on Barney's VRISE attributes, from the RBV perspective, (here high refers to a resource variable possessing four or more of Barney's attributes) and 2 the resources should have statistical significance in any of the regression models of this study as presented in table 6.24 in chapter six.

Table 7.1 presents a matrix showing the status of various independent resource variables used in this study in the VRISE framework, as well as their significance ratio, and the nature of their effect on school performance. In table 7.1, the "significant ratio" is represented as the number of times an independent resource variable was significant, divided by total number of regression models in which it was entered. Table 7.1 shows that three resource variables: flush toilets, electricity, and English language teachers were the strongest predictors on school performance in terms of significance ratio and also possessed four of the Barney's VRISE attributes. In addition, while these resource variables were also partially substitutable, they were not entirely so.

Table 7.1
Interpretation of Findings Based on RBV/VRISE Theoretical Framework

Type		Variable	Valuable?	Rare?	Costly to Imitate?	Non-substitutable?	Exploitable?	Significance ratio	Effect	Magnitude of effect
Control	1	Quality of students	√	X	X	√	√	7/8	+	Mixed
	2	School level	√	X	√	√	√	1/8	-	Strong
	3	Prior students' achievement	√	X	X	X	√	1/8	+	Strong
Financial	1	School revenue	√	√	X	X	√	1/4	-	Strong
	2	Filing revenue reports	√	√	√	√	√	3/4	-	Mixed
	3	Past loans	√	√	X	X	√	None	N/A	N/A
Physical	1	Library use	√	√	√	√	√	1/4	-	Weak
	2	Flushing toilets	√	√	√	√*	√	4/4	-	Strong
	3	Internet connection	√	√	√	√	√	1/4	-	Weak
	4	Science laboratory	√	√	√	X	√	None	N/A	N/A
	5	Buildings with glass	√	√	√	X	√	None	N/A	N/A
	6	Electricity	√	√	√	√*	√	4/4	-	Mixed
	7	Entertainment provision	√	√	X	X	√	None	-	N/A
	8	Student/book ratio	√	X	X	X	√	2/4	-	Mixed
Human	1	Examiner ratio	√	√	√	√	√	None	N/A	N/A
	2	Markers contracted ratio	√	√	√	√	√	None	N/A	N/A
	3	Boarding student ratio	√	X	√	X	√	3/4	-	Mixed
	4	English teacher ratio	√	√	√	√*	√	4/4	-	Strong
	5	Maths teacher ratio	√	√	√	√*	√	None	N/A	N/A
	6	Teacher/student- ratio	√	X	√	X	√	None	N/A	N/A

√ = Yes meaning no alternative; X = No meaning available alternative; √* = Yes meaning alternative exists but does not meet required or expected stan dard

Flush Toilets

The notion that having flush toilets is strongly related to school performance seems initially perplexing. Using the lens of the RBV some plausible, but speculative explanations for the unusual, but statistically strong, relationships of flush toilets and school performance are presented.

In many developing countries, flush toilets are resources that remain valuable, rare, and difficult to imitate. Consequently most secondary schools cannot afford to duplicate these resources. In the developing countries' context, installation of flush toilets is extremely costly, among other things due to the fact that not only are the toilets themselves extremely costly, but they require large amounts of water, incur significantly more "out flow" capabilities than traditional "pit latrines," and have much higher maintenance costs than more common alternatives. Flush toilets, then, proxy for a much larger water infrastructure than most schools can possibly create or maintain. In Sub-Saharan Africa, a highly developed water infrastructure is indeed a rare thing. Thus many secondary schools lacking sufficient financial backing or financial strength (Barney, 1986) are constrained from implementing such unique critical resources. While flush toilets are simply taken as given in most secondary schools of industrialized countries, such resources are unique and extremely hard to find in most developing countries.

The few secondary schools that possess these unique resources enjoyed competitive advantage over the other schools that did not have these particular resources and facilities. What actually confounds the whole picture is that while flush toilets are partially substitutable, they are not in any sense transferable or tradable (Grant, 1991). Given that richer parents and their students may prefer secondary schools that offer better hygienic conditions and other high priority conditions affiliated with a developed water infrastructure, with the effect of attracting larger students' enrolments that could facilitate benefits associated with economies of scale. In addition, these conditions might function as non - remunerated incentives for better qualified teachers to work for schools that offer the cleaner and more amenable environments created in schools with flush toilets and all that they imply.

Clearly, since so many "collateral" resources are required to facilitate flush toilets, the presence of this resource might actually be considered as a proxy for many other important resources. It is not uncommon for proxy measures to mask the existence of other equally important resources. The analysis in this study did not indicate what these other "proxy" resources might be, but it is not an unwarranted assertion that other unmeasured resources are implied by the existence of a highly developed water infrastructure. A need exists for follow-up studies to address such potentially confounding conditions.

Electricity

This study has indicated that electricity scores high on Barney's VRISE attributes. Similar to flush toilets, electricity as a resource is valuable, rare, difficult to imitate, and is only partially substitutable in many developing countries. Installation of electricity in a secondary school is extremely expensive and many schools cannot afford it. Successful installation of electricity in a school may not necessarily guarantee regular and reliable service. Some secondary schools that are connected to electrical sources often spend months without any actual flow of electricity. While some schools may improvise with alternative power sources, such as generators, to fill in when electricity goes out, these alternatives are inadequate and sometimes even unacceptable due to high operational costs and fluctuations in electrical voltage flow (which may damage delicate and expensive systems).

If one school has a reliable regular main electric power supply and its neighboring school does not, electricity becomes non-transferable and non-tradable between those schools. As indicated in the analysis, a school with reliable regular electric power supply will enjoy significant competitive advantage over the other school. Since students learn better in classrooms with sufficient and predictable lighting, students attending well-lit schools are most likely to learn better than those in other schools with inadequate lighting facilities (Benya, 2001; Caillods & Postlethwaite, 1995; Jago & Tanner, 1999). This finding is consistent with RBV perspective because schools connected to a unique resource (electricity) tended to out perform other schools in UCE examinations.

English Language Teachers

This study has indicated that English language teachers are high on Barney's VRISE attributes. Thus, English language teachers are extremely valuable, rare, difficult to duplicate, and only partially substitutable. This study has further revealed that the "percentage of English language teachers" variable (a human resource) was by far the highest predictor of school performance.

This finding suggests that increasing the number of English language teachers in a secondary school in Mukono District, in Uganda will be associated with higher performance in UCE examinations. Given that English is the medium of instruction in teaching pedagogy and curriculum, teachers of English language are considered extremely critical resources. Yet, the findings of this study showed that teachers of English language were too few in proportion to the secondary schools in Mukono District, in Uganda to circulate around the market or to be shared or traded among all schools. Therefore, it is not surprising that secondary schools with more English language teachers tended to out perform other schools in UCE examinations. This finding is also consistent with RBV perspective.

In the school context of Mukono District, in Uganda some resource variables seem to be inconsistent with the RBV perspective. The following section discusses a few of these resource variables that seem to be incommensurable with the RBV perspective.

APPARENT INCONSISTENCIES WITH THE RBV

In table 7.1 some resources variables that seem to be incommensurable with the RBV perspective are identified, yet these resource variables were high on Barney's VRISE attributes: examiners, markers, and teachers of Mathematics. Irrespective of these resource variables being high on Barney's VRISE attributes, they did not show any statistical significance in any of the regression models in this study. This finding suggests that, perhaps, these independent resource variables were less important in school performance, which might be quite misleading and inconsistent with RBV. In the theoretical sense, these resource variables were actually supposed to be important even though they were not significant and RBV theorists would have expected them to have stronger effect on performance. Consequently, this finding may confound the researcher's ability to sufficiently discern the actual effect of these particular independent resource variables in the variations in school performance in UCE examinations.

Nonetheless, drawing on the RBV theoretical framework, the discrepancies observed in some of the resource variables in this study could be explained. In order to understand why these discrepant variables did not affect school performance, even though RBV would suggest they should, this discussion must pay particular attention to the concepts of resource sharing and overcoming resource barriers. These two concepts seem to have profound influence on resource access, utilization, and performance of secondary schools in Mukono District, in Uganda

Resource Sharing

An organization attempting to protect and maintain its superior performance position must safeguard its advantage creating resources from easy access to potential competitors. However, this study highlights an unprecedented or at least previously unidentified resource sharing culture demonstrated by secondary schools in Mukono District, in Uganda. These schools have used resource sharing as one of the strategies to tap into the critical advantage creating resources of other schools to achieve their goals and objectives (Hitt, Ireland, et al., 2001).

Resource sharing appears to be facilitated in schools in Mukono District, in Uganda through the formation of strategic alliances and networks among school administrators (J. M. Hite, et al., 2002; Hitt, Ireland, et al., 2001), and through existing goodwill and trust established over time, that is social capital (Burt, 1992). By doing so, increased resource sharing appears to be leading to reduced heterogeneity among schools in terms of those shared resources which subsequently narrows the performance gaps between partner schools basing on these particular resources. Additionally, establishing and maintaining organizational structures to permit efficient sharing of critical resources or assets that are relevant to more than one school would not necessarily lead to sustainable superior performance (Markides & Williamson, 1996), but would profoundly boost the overall average performance of all partner schools involved in the network. An important policy question that remains unanswered is: What are the consequences of resource sharing in terms of improving or retarding educational quality, especially when resources are spread too thin among all partner schools? This question requires further research.

Overcoming Resource Barriers

Some organizations strategically improve their survival by overcoming resource barriers. In the real world of competition, organizations tend to create resources barriers to protect their advantage creating resources, thus prohibiting other competing organizations from gaining easy access to those unique resources. On the basis of this research, it appears that many secondary schools in Mukono District, in Uganda have done the contrary. These schools have leveraged their critical advantage creating resources through the removal of resource barriers and resource sharing. Hitt, Ireland, and Hoskisson (2001) point out that:

> Inadequate resources, whether financial, technical, or important capabilities, have forced firms [schools] to form alliances to compete in specific markets. Thus, the primary reason for strategic alliances is the opportunity for partners to share resources. Also alliances help firms acquire certain types of resources. For instance, firms may enhance their capabilities by learning from partners, thereby improving their resource base (p. 196).

Subsequently, overcoming resource barriers and resource sharing becomes a reasonable strategy, especially in conditions of abysmal poverty common in developing countries where schools cannot afford to acquire every vital critical advantage creating resource they need to accomplish all their educational programs. Returning to the prior question of whether the non-statistically significant resources that are also high on the VRISE scale violates the RVB model, we must ask the salient question of how the failure to show any statistical significance by some of the shared critical resources across competing secondary schools in Mukono District, in Uganda could be interpreted to preserve the sense of RBV relevance as a consistent and sufficient explanatory framework.

Interpretation of Apparent RBV Inconsistencies

This study asserts that the concept of resource sharing and overcoming resource barriers renders advantage - creating resources more homogeneous among partner schools. Hence, in turn, variability across schools in terms of heterogeneous services offered by schools is lowered. For instance, many schools can gain access to resources of the tacit knowledge and skills of specialized teachers (markers, examiners, and science teachers) as these resources are contracted out by schools previously advantaged by exclusive access to these resources. Therefore, such resource sharing might be a plausible explanation as to why these critical resource variables (according to the VRISE analysis) turned out to be weak predictors in all regression models of this study. When specialized teachers are contracted out by other competitor schools, their advantage - creating potential is eroded or distributed, even though in a non - contextualized sense their "individual skills may be highly tacit, making them inimitable and non - substitutable" (Fahy, 2000, p. 98). In other words, all secondary schools seem to enjoy relatively similar services from those specialized teachers being shared or contracted across competitor schools. Thus, these circumstances are likely to decrease the probability that some resource variables will emerge as statistically significant, even though from the RBV perspective they are inimitable and non - substitutable.

By and large when schools become more homogeneous and less heterogeneous in terms of critical resources, the likelihood of the influence of these critical resources (in the general VRISE sense) on school performance is consequently lowered. Therefore, recognizing and accounting for the role of resource heterogeneity in education production becomes extremely critical. With this critical caution in mind, RBV offers even greater promise in terms of interpretive power than the traditional production function commonly used in education because a resource does not need to emerge as simply statistically significant to be of importance in an analytical and policy sense. This issue is dealt with in the following section.

BEYOND THE PRODUCTION FUNCTION MODEL

In order to understand why, based on this study, the RBV offers greater interpretive power than the production function model so dominant in historical educational literature, it is prudent to briefly look at the assumptions and limitations of the production function model itself. In essence, this study provides a rationale of how and why RBV could be used to extend and bridge the existing knowledge beyond the production function model about the relationship between school resources and school performance.

Assumptions of "Production Function"

The production function model is a technical device dealing with the relationships between the inputs and outputs of a school or educational system. The production function model in its simplest form could be represented by the following equation:

$$\hat{Y} = f(X)$$

In this simplified equation, Y refers to outputs such as skills attained and performance in exit examinations. X refers to inputs such as capital, labor, financial, human, or physical resources and f indicates that a change or a manipulation in X will lead to a corresponding and predictable change in $\hat{Y}$.

The production function in education works on the assumption that educational institutions function like factories (Belfield, 2000). That is, if X resource inputs are supplied into the educational process, these resource inputs can be rationally, directly, and predictably transformed into $\hat{Y}$ educational performance outcomes. The production function further implies that, keeping other factors equal, if X resource inputs are doubled then $\hat{Y}$ performance outcomes will double (Nicholson, 1998). This perspective suggests that if one knows the resource inputs entering into the education production process, then one could predict the expected educational performance outcomes. Therefore, educational production processes should be easily and predictably replicated in different schools, providing similar resource inputs are made available to all schools, resulting in similar if not identical outcomes (Fidalgo & Garcia, 2003; P. Lewin, 2004).

Furthermore, the production function is also based on the assumption that decision-making processes are homogeneous for all educational institutions and that administrators and teachers act rationally with their main motive as ensuring efficient optimization of resources in the education production processes (Nicholson, 1998). Based on this view, all people involved in the education production processes presumably work efficiently and rationally to maximize educational performance outcomes (for the attainment of technical efficiency). The assumptions of homogeneity in decision making processes and rational motives in the optimization of resources create a condition labeled "technical efficiency" in the production function model.

However, technical efficiency quite often falls short in the real world of the educational process. Given that lack of technical efficiency is often found in many education systems of developing countries, those systems and governments, and/or the individuals in either, are often criticized for being inefficient and ineffective (Harber & Davies, 1997). Due to the predictable violations of the assumption of technical efficiency, the notion of continuing to apply the production function model in the educational systems of developing countries has become fundamentally untenable.

Limitations of the Production Function in Education

Fidalgo and Garcia (2003) pointed out that production function theorists disregard the reasonable possibility and impact of institutional and individual behavior that leads toward inefficiency. These theorists insist that individuals involved in decision making and implementation of educational goals execute them as planned without any significant variations or discrepancies. In this theoretical scenario, nothing unexpected would happen and none of the plans would fail (P. Lewin, 2004). However, this view is likely to be found a fallacy in the complex and socially-embedded world of real education production processes because "sub optimal decision making and resource wasting seem to happen in real [education] production processes" (Fidalgo & Garcia, 2003, p. 4). Given that school managers and teachers often have vested interests or hidden personal agendas, may lack information, or may be incompetent, schools in developing countries often do not make the best use of available resources, which leads to conflict with the principle of technical efficiency.

To confound the potential utility of production function thinking even further, it is important to consider that although many factors of the education production process might be heterogeneous, intangible and non-measurable they could still be influential in a real and practical sense. Thus, another shortcoming of the production function model is its failure to pay particular attention to heterogeneous, intangible and non-measurable resource factors.

According to Monk (1992) another limitation of the production function model is its failure to model the changeable nature of the educational process. Simply disregarding the changeable nature of educational processes and maintaining the presumption of the existence of a state of equilibrium is a serious oversight. As P. Lewin (2004) convincingly stated:

> The limitations of the production function framework are
> related also to its existence inside an equilibrium world.
> It is in equilibrium that the production function is presumed
> to represent knowledge that is available not only to the theorist
> but also, in some way, to the economic agents of the model.
> The outputs are assumed to follow a technically known way
> from the application of inputs and the value of the outputs
> is likewise known, so that the inputs can be paid the
> unambiguous value of their marginal products (p. 14).

As Lewin has indicated, clearly the production function theory tends to be a predictive tool, which works best under stable, equalized conditions. However, given that educational processes are increasingly influenced by rapidly changing and diverse educational goals, cultural differences, and political backgrounds (Spencer & Wiley, 1981), a phenomenon of disequilibrium has become the more realistic and substantial reality in education. Presuming the existence of equilibrium at all times (P. Lewin, 2004) is increasingly inconsistent, questionable, and unacceptable in the real context of education in developing countries. Consequently, over-reliance on the production function in studies and policy making in education is extremely problematic and increasingly untenable (P. Lewin, 2004). In this book I suggest RBV as a potential powerful tool that could be used to extend further the school resources and performance research efforts. This is elaborated further in the remaining sections, but offers ground for further research.

THE RBV SOLUTION

The RBV recognizes that resource heterogeneity allows different organizations to achieve different levels of performance outcomes from tangible inputs, thereby generating outcomes that could lead to sustainable competition (Barney, 1991a; Fidalgo & Garcia, 2003). Fidalgo and Garcia (2003) point out that "given the concept of resource heterogeneity, firms [that is, schools] ... operate on different production frontiers" (p. 12). Schools and educational settings are heterogeneous because they are different in terms of their particularistic mix of resource endowments, socio-cultural contexts, and compositions of leaders and teachers with varying technical competencies and priorities.

This heterogeneity of resources, organizational contexts, and institutional behaviors are important components of the educational process that could account for much of the outcome inefficiency manifest in research in the field (Fidalgo & Garcia, 2003). It could even be rationally asserted that two schools with similar resources, contexts and behaviors could come up with completely heterogeneous services and outcomes (Penrose, 1959).

Practical Policy Implications and Future Research Directions

Providing quality education, improving access to education, and making education more affordable to less-privileged youth living under increasingly shrinking resources remains the critical challenge encountered by policy makers and educators in developing countries. In these circumstances, policy makers are seriously constrained in identifying, investing, and nurturing critical resources that best contribute on student performance. Without reliable and valid research-based information on available critical resources in schools, efforts to enable schools to make the best use of the local available critical resources will remain unfounded and largely ineffective. In the following section, some policy implications based on the research conducted in this study are highlighted and discussed.

Policy Implications

This study identified three key policy implications from the research and analysis: Use of satellite schools; School location and resources; and Training and deployment of highly qualified English language teachers in schools.

Satellite schools: This study revealed that secondary schools in Mukono District, in Uganda have succeeded in competing favorably, irrespective of their weak financial strength and lack of critical resources, through resource sharing and overcoming resource barriers. One policy that could be implemented to take advantage of this finding would be one that would encourage the creation of a formal system of satellite schools. A system of satellite schools is in line with the concepts of resource sharing and overcoming resource barrier identified in this research and presented earlier in this chapter. The policy driven possibilities of using a system of satellite schools in developing countries presents important and positive policy implications based on the findings of this study. A central school, established, furnished, and supplied with the essential critical resources identified in this study, which could then share those resources with satellite schools strategically located in a reasonably proximate geographical area could serve and support teachers, and students in the satellite schools. Obviously, not all critical resources identified in this study can be shared. Particularly challenging in this regard are flush toilets, and to a lesser degree electricity. But certainly English language teachers could be easily shared to great collective advantage, and perhaps some of the infrastructure amenities implied by the other two resources could be identified and shown to be "sharable," tradable or substitutable to some degree by future research efforts.

Given the paucity of resources across secondary schools in developing countries, it would be fundamentally cheaper, much more cost effective and cost efficient to equip and furnish one strategically positioned "central" or "hub" school with all the basic critical resources for collective use, rather than spreading those same resources too thinly among all the schools to little or no collective benefit. The notion of a satellite school system should and ought to be encouraged, facilitated, and embraced by policy makers and government ministries in developing countries. Through such efforts contemporary secondary schools in developing countries may improve their performance and educational quality. Further inquiry into the practicability of this model and possibilities for its adoption by schools in developing countries is needed.

Locating schools and resources: Without actually knowing where schools are literally located and what current critical resources they either have or lack, how could policy makers and educational planners be expected to appropriately and effectively plan for schools? This study revealed that most secondary schools are located near the main roads. The findings of this study suggest that the strategic location of a school is important and may influence the kind of resources the school is able to procure and maintain.

Further research on why and how school proximity to roads contributes to better performance needs to be conducted. This can help extend our understanding on how strategic locations of schools may influence their future resource acquisition as well affecting their performance.

Training and deployment of highly qualified English language teachers: This study has revealed that of all the human resource variables English language teachers are by far the strongest predictors on school performance. Policy makers and educational planners must realize the need to focus on training and deployment of enough highly qualified English language teachers in all secondary schools, either through a satellite system as previously described or in some other fashion within the financial limits of the national educational budget.

In addition, this policy implication entails the need to provide in-service training to current teachers of English. This is particularly true of those teaching English but are not trained or qualified to do so. The bottom line of the findings in this study, in this regard is the critical and pressing need to re - evaluate language policy and practices in the Ugandan education system.

Recommendations for Future Research

In addition to those recommendations already given in the previous section, the following two general suggestions also deserve consideration:

First, Sergiovanni (1984, p. 9) pointed out that "cultural life in schools is constructed reality." Some of the secondary schools in Mukono District, in Uganda have already informally set up a cultural arrangement that facilitates the leveraging of some critical resources through resource sharing. This previously unidentified informal system of a resource sharing culture in secondary schools in Mukono District, in Uganda confounds traditional inferential analysis, such as production function analysis, that can be made basing on the effect of quantity and quality of resources available on school performance. A critical need exists for further research to examine the underlying factors of how the informal sharing of critical resources among secondary schools in Mukono District, in Uganda can be formalized in such a way that the prevailing environment of stiff competition among those schools does not hamper or minimize broad scale benefit to the needy students in the country. More specifically, there is need to address questions such as: What are the pros and cons of resource sharing and its impact on secondary school performance? How can the practice of resource sharing be enhanced and formalized to influence the overall quality of education? What traditional notions of inter - school resource competition can be utilized in developing a positive and collective culture of resource sharing?

Secondly, this study also revealed that a few schools were persistent outliers in terms of performance in UCE examination scores over the four year period (2000-2003) included in the data set. There is need to understand the particular factors that create persistent school performance outliers. Examining whether substantial differences exist in ways persistent high and low performing schools utilize their resources compared to other schools seems critical. This would unfold and generate valuable knowledge to enable a better conceptualization of the relationship between resources performance of schools with traditions of low or high performance. Often, inquiry is limited either to only one end of the spectrum or another and most often on only those which are the best performing. This anomaly seems odd that research does not frame work in terms of both extremes to formulate better notions of the true range of educational performance in formulating conclusions and policy responses.

GENERAL CONCLUSIONS

This work has presented groundbreaking research exploring the relationship between educational resources and secondary school performance in Mukono District, in Uganda. The results were interpreted through the RBV theoretical framework. This study has revealed mixed findings on the effect of various financial, physical and human resource variables on school performance. English language teachers proved to be the strongest predictor on school performance. Surprisingly, a few resource variables such as percentage of markers, examiners, and mathematics teachers found to be high on Barney's VRISE framework, did not show any statistical significance in any of the regression models. The analysis showed that statistical insignificance is more likely when critical resources become more homogeneous across secondary schools. It appears that in some instances this homogeneity is often associated with schools sharing some critical resources. However, it should be pointed out that lack of statistical significance does not necessarily imply lack of importance of a particular resource variable in terms of practical value and policy application/utility.

This work proposes that contemporary secondary schools in the developing world could be well advised to explore and perhaps embrace a system that encourages symbiotic relationships among themselves, between richer and poorer schools, in terms of resource sharing and networking of vital information geared toward improving the quality of education.

LESSONS LEARNED THROUGH THIS STUDY

First, while good data is important and good technique or methodology is critical in any research endeavor, good interpretive tools and frameworks, are the primary key for useful and meaningful research efforts. Recognizing that good methodology precedes the gathering of good data and that good data is vital to provide the basis for interpretation, good interpretive tools entail a good theoretical framework or paradigm, which unfolds and directs what researchers perceive to be acceptable knowledge, to attach meaning to data, and to enable the researcher to make significant and defensible interpretations of the data and analyses.

Subsequently, good data and good methodology are insufficient without a sound interpretive theoretical framework because without recourse to an accepted framework the researcher is constrained from what he/she can see from the data and what conclusions he/she can make. Additionally, without recourse to an accepted and respected framework, detractors are free to employ whatever competing or detracting interpretations they might put forward. In lieu of the use of an accepted framework, any person involved in the discourse is free and unrestricted, and what interpretations or policies are proposed depends mainly upon the paradigmatic community to which one belongs (Kuhn, 1996). While educational researchers deserve and ought to use rigorous acceptable scientific methods to generate good data, most importantly they must employ a rigorous and sound interpretive theoretical framework to that data in order to address the dynamic and complex problems of education that are nested within a world of competing and often conflicting paradigms and interpretive frameworks.

Secondly, this study contributes to knowledge in that while the quantity and quality of resources are important, knowledge of resources *per se* is not sufficient without knowing how these resources are used, particularly in developing countries (Barney, 2002; Inkeles, 1979; Ray, Barney, & Muhanna, 2004) . By and large, donor agencies have provided educational resources to schools in developing countries for decades, but many of these resources have not made substantial differences in terms of improving educational quality. Most of these critical resources do not usually find their way effectively into classroom instruction simply because teachers and administrators do not know how to use them effectively. Vignette 2 presented a typical example that highlighted a high school in Uganda, which received five new computers from USA and never used them. Furthermore, without resources being transformed into something useful in an educational and competitive sense, however good a resource may be considered to be, it cannot contribute to school performance in a predictable and replicable way. Policy makers must pay particular attention to ensure that practitioners in schools know how to use the available resources.

Thirdly, this study further adds to the knowledge that advantage-creating resources must be identified and understood in the current resource poor but highly competitive setting in developing countries. Clearly, one cannot effectively and efficiently utilize a resource that is not known to him or her. Quite often teachers may not even know what resources are available, let alone knowing which resources are truly the most critical.

On their part, school managers may also find it difficult to identify critical advantage creating resources in their institutions. Therefore the need exists to identify, invest, and nurture a clear knowledge of advantage creating resources that are accessible to school managers. Perhaps a confounding paradox is that often what appears to work best for one school or one set of students may not work for another school or set of students, depending largely on the schools' specific context.

Fourthly, Schools must look beyond their own gates for advantage creating resources that can be shared with other schools as a way to survive the stiff competitive environment common today in developing countries. This notion of knowing what advantage creating resources other schools have, and which of those they can or cannot be shared is critical. Schools must avoid thinking that leads them to conclude that they are unavoidably "getting stuck with what they have and living with what they lack" (Teece, et al., 1990, p. 8). This is a common tendency, which prohibits innovation and limits expansion, and undermines the improvement performance in the rapidly changing society of globalization as well.

CONCLUSIONS

This study has demonstrated that RBV has the potential of bridging the knowledge gap in educational productivity based on critical resources. Given the key RBV assumptions of resource heterogeneity and resource immobility, the RBV offers greater interpretive power compared to the more traditional production function model. This study proposes that the RBV is a marked interpretive improvement to the more traditional but highly embattled possibilities presented by the production function approach. This work has opened a new door in demonstrating how the application of the RBV framework to an analysis of potentially critical educational resources can have a positive effect at the secondary level on our understanding and proposing policies for the improvement of school performance and school effectiveness in a developing context.

The purpose of this book is to demonstrate how RBV could provide a useful theoretical framework in school resources and school performance research studies. The main goal was to provide insights on the RBV application in education, but more so to demonstrate how this relatively new theoretical perspective could used. This is a groundbreaking research in the field of school effectiveness and school resources. It will increasingly even become more relevant as schools are currently operating more like private business organization than as public service providers as the case was in 1960s', 70s' and 80s'.

REFERENCES

ADEA. (2003). *The challenge of Learning: Improving the quality of basic education in Sub-Saharan Africa.* Paper presented at the ADEA Biennial Meeting 2003, Grand, Baie, Mauritius, December 3-6.

Adekanmbi, G., Kamou, J., & Mphinyane, O. P. (1996). Collaboration in distance education. *Journal of the African Association for Literacy and Adult Education,* 10(1), 19-41.

Aim, E. M. (1972). *Resources for secondary education in Ontario: Their distribution and relationship to educational outputs.* Unpublished Dissertation, University of Toronto, Ontario.

Allison, P. D. (1999). *Multiple Regression: A Primer.* Thousands Oaks, CA: Pine Forge Press.

Alvarez, B., & Bradsher, M. (2003, 9-13 June 2003). *Beyond basic education-- Secondary education in the Developing World.* Paper presented at the SEIA, by Elizabeth Leu, The Academy for Educational Development and The World Bank Institute [AED] (New publication forthcoming), Kampala, Uganda.

Amis, J., Pant, N., & Slack, T. (1997). Achieving a sustainable competitive advantage: A resource-based view of sport sponsorship. *Journal of Sport Management,* 11, 80-96.

Amit, R., & Schoemaker, P. J. H. (1993). Strategic assets and organizational rent. *Strategic Management Journal,* 14, 33-46.

Anderson, S. E. (2002). The double mirrors of school improvement: The Aga khan Foundation in East Africa. In S. E. Anderson (Ed.), *Improving schools through teacher development: Case studies of the Aga Khan Foundation projects in East Africa* (pp. 1-19). Lisse: Swets & Zeitlinger Publishers.

Anderson, S. E., & Sumra, S. (2002). Building professional community at Mzizima secondary school, Tanzania. In S. E. Anderson (Ed.), *Improving schools through teacher development: Case studies of the Aga Khan Foundation projects in East Africa* (pp. 47-82). Lisse: Swets & Zeitlinger Publishers.

Atchoarena, D., & Hite, S. J. (2001). Lifelong learning policies in low development Context: An African perspective. In D. Aspin, J. Chapman, m. Hatton & Y. Sawano (Eds.), *International Handbook of lifelong learning* (pp.201-228). Dordrecht/Boston/London: kluwer Academic Publishers.

Barney, J. B. (1986). Strategic factor markets: Expectations, luck, and business strategy. *Management Science,* 32(10), 1231-1241.

Barney, J. B. (1989). Asset accumulation and the sustainability of competitive advantage. *Management Science,* 35(12), 1511-1513.

Barney, J. B. (1991a). Firm resources and sustained competitive advantage. *Journal of Management,* 17(1), 99-120.

Barney, J. B. (1991b). Special theory forum the Resource-Based Model of the firm: Origins, Implications, and prospects. *Journal of Management,* 17(1), 97-98.

Barney, J. B. (1996). The resource-based theory of the firm. *Organization Science,* 7(5), 469.

Barney, J. B. (2001a). Is the resource-based "view" a useful perspective for strategic management research? Yes. *Academy Of Management*

Review, 26(1), 41-56.

Barney, J. B. (2001b). Resource-based theories of competitive advantage: A ten-year retrospective on the resource-based view. Journal of Management, 27, 643-650.

Barney, J. B. (2002). Gaining and sustaining competitive advantage (2nd ed.). Upper Saddle River, NJ: Prentice-Hall, Inc.

Barney, J. B., & Arikan, A. M. (2001). The resource-based view: Origins and implications. In M. A. Hitt, R. E. Freeman & J. S. Harrison (Eds.), The Blackwell Handbook of strategic management (pp. 125-188). Oxford, UK: Malden MA: Blackwell Publishers, 2001.

Barney, J. B., & Wright, P. M. (1998). On becoming a strategic partner: The human resources in gaining competitive advantage. Human role of Resource Management, 37(1), 31-46.

Barney, J. B., & Zajac, E. J. (1994). Competitive organizational behavior: Toward an organizationally-based theory of competitive advantage. Strategic Management Journal, 15(Winter, 1994), 1-4.

Barro, R. J., & Lee, J. W. (2000). International data on educational attainment: Updates and implications (CID Working Paper No. 42). Boston: Center for International Development (CID) at Harvard University.

Bauer, A., Brust, F., & Hubbert, J. (2002). Expanding private education in Kenya: Mary Okelo and Mikini schools. Entrepreneurship: A case study in African enterprise growth. Chazen Web Journal of International Business, Fall 2002, 19.

Belfield, C. R. (2000). Economic principles for education. Cheltenham, UK: Edward Elgar.

Bennell, P., & Sayed, Y. (2002a). Improving the management and internal effeciency of post-primary education and training in Uganda. Kampala: Ministry of Education and Sports (MOES).

Bennell, P., & Sayed, Y. (2002b). Improving the management and internal efficiency of post-primary education and training in Uganda. Kampala: Ministry of Education and Sports (MOES).

Benya, J. (2001). Lighting for schools. Washington D. C.: National Clearinghouse for Educational Facilities.

Bienayme, A. (1995). Does company strategy have any lessons for educational planning? In J. Hallak & F. Caillods (Eds.), Educational planning : International dimension (pp. 259-271). New York & London: Garland Publishing, Inc.

Bliss, J. R. (1991). Strategic and holistic images of effective schools. In J. R. Bliss, W. A. Firestone & C. E. Richards (Eds.), Rethinking effective schools research and practice (pp. 43-57). Englewood Cliffs, New Jersey: Prentice Hall.

Bollen, R. (1996). School effectiveness and school improvement: The intellectual and policy context. In D. Reynolds, R. Bollen, B. Creemers, D. Hopkins, L. Stoll & N. Lagerweij (Eds.), Making good schools: Linking school effectiveness and school improvement (pp. 1-20). London and New York: Routledge.

Bosker, R. J., Creemers, B. P. M., & Stringfield, S. (1999). Enduring problems and changing conceptions. In R. J. Bosker, B. P. M. Creemers & S. Stringfield (Eds.), Enhancing educational excellency, equity and efficiency : Evidence from evaluations of systems and schools in

change. Dordrecht/Boston/London: Kluwer Academy Publishers.
Bourke, A. (2000). A model of the determinants of international trade in higher education. The Service of Industries Journal, 20(1), 110-138.
Bourque, L. B., & Fielder, E. P. (1995). How to conduct self-administered and mail surveys. Thousand Oaks, CA: SAGE Publications, Inc.
Bradshaw, Y. W. (1993). State limitation, self-help secondary schooling, and development in Kenya. Social Forces, 72(2), 347-378.
Bregman, J., & Stallmeister, S. (2001). Secondary education in Africa (SEIA): A Regional study of Africa Region of the World Bank: The World Bank SEIA Regional Office.
Bregman, J., & Stallmeister, S. (2002, May). Secondary education in Africa (SEIA): A regional study of the Africa Region of the World Bank. Paper presented at the Secondary education in Africa: Strategies for renewal, Mauritius.
Brewer, D. J., Krop, C., Gill, B. P., & Reichardt, R. (1999). Estimating the cost of National class size reductions under different policy alternatives. Educational Evaluation and Policy Analysis, 21(2), 179-192.
Brock, K. J. (2002). The novice researcher: Expectation meets reality. In G. Walford (Ed.), Doing a doctorate in educational ethnography (pp. 135-158). Amsterdam: JAI.
Burt, R. S. (1992). The social structure of competition. In N. Nohria & R. G. Eccles (Eds.), Networks and organizations: structure, form, and action (pp. 57-91). Boston, MA: Harvard Business School Press.
Caillods, F., & Lewin, K. M. (2001). Financing increased access and participation at secondary level: main policy options: Secondary education financing in Costa Rica: recovering the initiative. In K. M. Lewin & F. Caillods (Eds.), Financing secondary education in developing countries: Strategies for sustainable growth (pp. 283-355). Paris: UNESCO Publishing.
Caillods, F., & Postlethwaite, N. T. (1995). Teaching/learning conditions in developing countries. In J. Hallak & F. Caillods (Eds.), Educational planning: the international dimension (pp. 3-24). New York & London: Garlands Publishing, Inc.
Capon, N., Farley, J. U., & Hoenig, S. (1990). Determinants of financial performance: A meta-analysis. Management Science, 36(10), 1143-1159.
Card, D., & Krueger, A. B. (2000). School resources and student outcomes: An overview of the literature and new evidence from North and South Carolina. In A. B. Krueger (Ed.), Education matters: Selected essays (pp. 85-104). Northampton, Massachusetts: Edward Elgar Publishing Ltd.
Case, A., & Deaton, A. (1999). School inputs and educational outcomes in South Africa. The Quarterly Journal of Economics, 114(3), 1047-1084.
Chapman, D. W., & Mahlck, L. O. (1993). Improving educational quality through better use of information. Oxford: Pergamon Press.
Chapman, D. W., & Mulkeen, A. (2003). Selected findings from the review of literature on teacher recruitment, retention, and training in Africa (A part of World Bank/SEIA Thematic Study 4: Secondary school teachers and school principals): Academy for Educational Development [Forthcoming paper].
Cheng, Y. C. (1999). Recent education development in South East Asia: An introduction. School Effectiveness and School Improvement, 10(1), 3-9.
Chubb, J. E., & Moe, T. M. (1990). Politics, markets, and America's schools.

Washington, D. C.: The Brookings Institution.
CIDA. (2002). CIDA' action plan on basic education. Canada: Canadian International Development Agency.
Cleland, I. (1994). Networking quality: The issue is quality improvement. In P. Ribbins & E. Burridge (Eds.), Improving education: Promoting quality in schools (pp. 170-184). London: Cassell.
Cohen, D. K., Raudenbush, S. W., & Ball, D. L. (2003). Resources, instruction, and research. Educational Evaluation and Policy Analysis, 25(2), 119-142.
Cohn, E., Millman, S. D., & Chew, I.-K. (1975). Input-Output Analysis in public education. Cambridge: Ballinger Publishing Company.
Coleman, J. S., Campbell, E., Hobson, C., McPartland, J., Mood, A., Weinfeld, F., et al. (2000). The Coleman Report. In R. Arum & I. R. Beattie (Eds.), The structure of schooling: Readings in the sociology of education (pp. 154-167). Mountain View, California: Mayfield Publishing Company.
Coleman, J. S., Campbell, E. Q., Hobson, C. J., McPartland, J., Mood, A. M., Weinfeld, F. D., et al. (1966). Equality of educational opportunities. Washington: U. S. Government Printing Office.
Coleman, J. S., & Hoffer, T. (2000). Schools, families, and communities. In R. Arum & I. R. Beattie (Eds.), The structure of schooling: Readings in sociology of education (pp. 69-77). Mountain View, California: Mayfield Publishing Company.
Collis, D. J., & Montgomery, C. A. (1995). Competing on resources: Strategy in the 1990s. Harvard Business Review, 73(4), 118-129.
Conner, K. R. (1991). A historical comparison of resources-based theory and five schools of thought within industrial organization economics: Do we have a new theory of the firm? Journal of Management, 17(1), 121-154.
Conner, K. R., & Prahalad, C. K. (1996). A resource-based theory of the firm: Knowledge versus opportunism. Organization Science, 7(5), 477-501.
Cooper, B. S., Fusarelli, L. D., & Randall, E. V. (2004). Better policies better schools: Theories and applications. Boston: Pearson Education, Inc.
Cox, D., & Jimenez, E. (1997). The relative effectiveness of private and public schools: Evidence from two developing countries. In E. Cohn (Ed.), Market approaches to education: Vouchers and school choice (pp. 305-327). Oxford, UK: Pergamon.
Creemers, B. (1996). The goals of school effectiveness and school improvement. In D. Reynolds, R. Bollen, B. Creemers, D. Hopkins, L. Stoll & N. Lagerweij (Eds.), Making good schools: Linking school effectiveness and school improvement (pp. 21-58). London and New York: Routledge.
Dennison, B. (1990). The management of resources: Limited research effort on major issues. In R. Saran & V. Trafford (Eds.), Research in education management and policy (pp. 58-72). London: The Falmer Press.
Durand, R. (1999). The relative contributions of inimitable, non-transferable, and non-substitutable resources to profitability and market performance. In M. A. Hitt, R. D. Nixon, P. G. Clifford & K. P. Coyne (Eds.), Dynamic strategic resources: Development, diffusion and integration (pp. 67-95). Chichester-New York: John Wiley & Sons, ltd.
Edmonds, R. (1979). Effective schools for the urban poor. Educational Leadership, 37(October 1979), 15-24.
Fahy, J. (2000). The resource-based view of the firm: Some stumbling-blocks on the road to understanding sustainable competitive advantage.

Journal of European Industrial Training, 24(2/3/4), 94-105.

Fahy, J., & Smithee, A. (1999). Strategic marketing and the Resource Based View of the firm. Academy of Marketing Science Review, 10, 1-21.

Fertig, M. (2000). Old wine in new bottles? Researching effective schools in developing countries. School Effectiveness and School Improvement, 11(3), 385-403.

Fidalgo, E. G., & Garcia, A. C. (2003). A Resource-Based interpretation of technical efficiency indexes. Retrieved December 20th, 2003, from http://www19.uniovi.es/econo/doctrabajo/Dt01/d232_01.pdf

Figueredo, V., & Anzolone, S. (2003). Alternative models for secondary education in developing countries: Rationale and realities. The University of Pitsburgh: American Institute for Research in Collaboration with the Academy for Educational Development Education Development Center, Inc.

Firestone, W. A. (1991a). Educators, researchers, and the effective schools movement. In J. R. Bliss, W. A. Firestone & C. E. Richards (Eds.), Rethinking effective schools: Research and practice (pp. 12-27). Englewood Cliffs, New Jersey: Prentice Hall.

Firestone, W. A. (1991b). Introduction. In J. R. Bliss, W. A. Firestone & C. E. Richards (Eds.), Rethinking effective schools research and practice (pp. 1-11). Englewood Cliffs, New Jersey: Prentice Hall.

Foss, N. J. (2000). Equilibrium vs. evolution in the resource-based perspective: The conflict legacies of Demsetz and Penrose. In N. J. Foss, Robertson, P. L. (Ed.), Resources, technology and strategy: Explorations in the resource-based perspective (pp. 11-30). London: Routledge.

Foss, N. J. (2002). Edith Penrose, economics and strategic management. In C. Pitelis (Ed.), The growth of the firm (pp. 174-164). Oxford: Oxford University Press.

Fullan, M. (1997). What's worth fighting for in the principalship. New York: Teachers College Press.

Fullan, M., & Hargreaves, A. (1996). What's worth fighting for in your school. New York and London: Teacher's College press, University of Colombia.

Fuller, B. (1987). What school factors raise achievement in the Third World? Review of Educational Research, 57(3), 255-292.

Fuller, B., & Clarke, P. (1994). Raising school effects while ignoring culture? Local conditions and the influence of classroom tools, rules, and pedagogy. Review of Educational Research, 64(1), 119-157.

Fuller, B., & Heyneman, S. P. (1989). Third World school quality current collapse, future potential. Educational Researcher, 18(2), 12-19.

Fuller, B., Holsinger, D. B., Baker, D. P., Bellew, R., Bennett, R., Clarke, P., et al. (1993). Secondary education in developing countries (Discussion Paper Series No. 7). Washington D.C.: Education and Social Policy Department: The World bank.

Galvin, P. F. (1999). The politics of research on educational productivity. In B. S. Cooper & E. V. Randall (Eds.), Accuracy or advocacy: The politics of research in education (pp. 131-146). Thousand Oaks, California: Corwin Press, Inc.

Gannicott, K., & Throsby, D. (1998). Educational quality and effective schooling. In J. Delors (Ed.), Education for the twenty-first century: Issues and prospects (pp. 215-230): UNESCO Publishing.

Garfield, R., Holsinger, D. B., & Ziderman, A. (1994). The cost of secondary education expansion (ESP Discussion Paper Series No. 29). Washington D. C.: Education and Social Policy Department: The World Bank.

Gay, L. R., & Airasian, P. (2000). Educational research: Competencies for analysis and application (6th ed.). Columbus, Ohio: Merrill Publishing Company.

Grant, R. M. (1991). The resource-Based Theory of competitive advantage: Implication for strategy formulation. California Management Review, 33(3), 114-135.

Greenwald, R., Hedges, L. V., & Laine, R. D. (1996). Interpreting research on school resources and student achievement: A rejoinder to Hanushek. Review of Educational Research, 66(3), 411-416.

Gyimah-Brempong, K. (2003, January 2003). A review of education policy in Africa. Retrieved Dec. 5th, 2003, from www.dpmf.org/bulletin-jan-03/review-kwebena.html

Hallak, J. (1990). Investing in the future: Setting educational priorities in the developing world. Paris: UNESCO/IIEP, Pergamon Press.

Hallak, J., & Caillods, F. (1995). Introduction. In J. Hallak & F. Caillods (Eds.), Educational planning (pp. Ix-xvi). New York & London: Garlands Publishing, Inc.

Hanushek, E. A. (1981). Throwing money to schools. Journal of Policy Analysis and Management, 1(1), 19-41.

Hanushek, E. A. (1986). The economics of schooling: Production and efficiency in public schools. Journal of Economic Literature, 24(3), 1141-1177.

Hanushek, E. A. (1989). The impact of differential expenditures on school performance. Educational Researcher, 18(4), 45-51.

Hanushek, E. A. (1995). Interpreting recent research on schooling in developing countries. The World Bank Research Observer, 10(2), 227-246.

Hanushek, E. A. (1996). School resources and student performance. In G. Burtless (Ed.), Does money matter: The effect of school resources on student achievement and adult success (pp. 43-73). Washington D. C.: Brockings.

Hanushek, E. A. (1997). Assessing the effects of school resources on student performance: An update. Educational Evaluation and Policy Analysis, 19(2), 141-164.

Hanushek, E. A. (2003a). The failure of input-based schooling policies. The Economic Journal, 113(February), F64-F98.

Hanushek, E. A. (2003b). The importance of school quality (DP0HPETRI0500 No. rev1): Hoover Press: Peterson/Schools.

Hanushek, E. A., & Luque, J. A. (2002). Efficiency and equity in schools around the world (NBER working paper series No. 8949). Cambridge, MA: National Bureau of Economics Research.

Hanushek, E. A., Rivkin, S. G., & Taylor, L. L. (1996). Aggregation and the estimated effects of school resources. The Review of Economics and Statistics, 78(4), 611-627.

Harber, C., & Davies, L. (1997). School management and effectiveness in developing countries. London: Cassell.

Harber, C., & Muthukrishna, N. (2000). School effectiveness and school improvement in context: The case of South Africa. School Effectiveness and

School Improvement, 11(4), 421-434.
Harbison, R. W., & Hanushek, E. A. (1992). Educational performance of the poor: lesson from northeast Brazil. Washington, DC.: The international Bank for Reconstruction and Development/The World Bank.
Hargreaves, A., & Fullan, M. (1998). What's worth fighting for out there. New York London: Teacher's College Press, Colombia University.
Harris, A. M., & Dzinyela, J. M. (1997). Fostering English language learning in Ghana: Improving Educational Quality (IEQ) Project. Washington D. C.
Hedges, L., Laine, R. D., & Greenwald, R. (1994). Does money matter? A meta-analysis of studies of the effects of differential school inputs on student outcomes. Educational Researcher, 23(3), 5-14.
Hernes, G. (2001). Preface. In K. Lewin & F. Caillods (Eds.), Financing secondary education in developing countries: Strategies for sustainable growth (pp. v-vi). Paris: UNESCO Publishing.
Herpen, M. V. (1992). Conceptual models in use for education indicators. In N. Bottani & H. J. Walberg (Eds.), The OECD international education indicators (pp. 25-51). Paris: OECD publications.
Heyneman, S. P., & Loxley, W. A. (1982). Influences on academic achievement across high and low income countries: A re-analysis of IEA data. Sociology of Education, 55(1), 13-21.
Heyneman, S. P., & Loxley, W. A. (1983). The effect of primary-school quality on academic achievement across twenty-nine high-and low-income countries. American Journal of Sociology, 88(6), 1162-1194.
Hill, P. T., & Guthrie, J. W. (1999). A new research paradigm for understanding (And improving) Twenty-First Century. In J. Murphy & K. S. Louis (Eds.), Handbook of research on educational administration (2nd ed., pp. 511-523). San Francisco: Jossey-Bass Publishers.
Hite, J. M., Hite, S. J., Mugimu, C. B., Rew, J. W., & Nsubuga, Y. (2004, March 10th,). Making the grade: Using student national exams scores in school evaluation. Paper presented at the 48th Annual Conference, Comparative and International Education Society, Salt Lake City, Utah, USA.
Hite, J. M., Hite, S. J., Rew, J. W., Mugimu, C. B., & Nsubuga, Y. (2004, March 10th,). On the road to school effectiveness and efficiency: An inventory of school resources in 74 Ugandan secondary schools. Paper presented at the 48th annual Conference of the Comparative and International Education Society, Salt Lake City, Utah, USA.
Hite, J. M., Hite, S. J., Rew, W. J., Mugimu, B. C., & Nsubuga, Y. (2003). What's in a School? Financial, physical and human resources of Ugandan secondary schools.Unpublished manuscript, Salt Lake City, UT.
Hite, J. M., Mugimu, C. B., & Hite, S. J. (2002). Improving resource acquisition for private schools in Uganda: The role and structure of strategic networks. Educational Magazine, 3(2), 9-13.
Hite, S. J. (2001). Reviewing research literature for policy development purposes. In K. N. Ross (Ed.), Educational fundamentals: Quantitative research methods for planning the quality of education. Paris, France: UNESCO/IIEP.
Hitt, M. A., Bierman, L., Shimizu, K., & Kochhar, R. (2001). Direct and moderating effects of human capital on strategy and performance in professional service firms: A Resource-Based Perspective. Academy of Management Journal, 44(1), 13-28.

Hitt, M. A., Ireland, R. D., & Hoskisson, R. E. (2001). Strategic management competitiveness and globalization. Versailles, KY: South-Western College Publishing Thomson Learning.

Holsinger, D. B., & Cowell, R. N. (2000). Positioning secondary school education in developing countries. Paris: IIEP/UNESCO.

Holsinger, D. B., Mugimu, C. B., & Jacob, J. (2001, March, 2001). Private secondary education: An analysis of costs, benefits and government policy. Paper presented at the Comparative and International Education Society, 14 March 2001, Washington, D. C.

Inkeles, A. (1979). National differences in scholastic performance. Comparative Education Review, 23(3), 386-407.

Jago, E., & Tanner, K. (1999). Affects of the school facilities on student achievement - visual (lighting and color). Retrieved July 28th, 2004, from http://www.coe.uga.edu/sdpl/researchabstracts/visual.html

Janssens, F. J. G., & Leeuw, F. L. (2001). Schools make a difference, but each difference is different: On Dutch schools and educational equality: Trends and challenges. Peabody Journal of Education, 76(3 & 4), 41-56.

Jencks, C., Smith, M., Acland, H., Bane, M. J., Cohen, D., Gintis, H., et al. (1972a). Inequality: A reassessment of the effect of family and schooling in America. New York: Basic Books, Inc., Publishers.

Jencks, C., Smith, M., Acland, H., Bane, M. J., Cohen, D., Gintis, H., et al. (1972b). Inequality: A reassessment of the effect of family and schooling in America. New York: Basic Books, Inc., Publishers.

Jencks, C., Smith, M., Acland, H., Bane, M. J., Cohen, D., Gintis, H., et al. (2000). Inequality in educational attainment. In R. Arum & I. R. Beattie (Eds.), The structure of schooling: readings in the sociology of education (pp. 168-181). Mountain View, California: Mayfield Publishing Company.

Jimenez, E., & Sawada, Y. (2001). Public for private: the relationship between public and private school enrollment in the Philippines. Economics of Education Review, 20, 389-399.

Jimenez, L. J. P., & Pinzon, A. R. (1999). School inputs in secondary education and their effects on academic achievement: A study in Colombia (LCSHD Paper Series No. 36): Human Development Department: The World Bank Latin America and the Caribbean Regional Office.

Jugdev, K., & Thomas, J. (2002). Project management maturity models: The silver bullets of competitive advantage? Project Management Journal, 33(4), 4-14.

Kajubi, P. W. S. (1992). Government white paper on implementation of the recommendations of the report of educationb policy review entitled "Education for national integrationb and development". Kampala, Uganda: Ministry of Education: Government of Uganda.

Kajubi, S. (1992). The Government White Paper on implementation of the recommendations of the report of education policy review entitled "Education for national integration and development". Kampala, Uganda: Ministry of Education: Government of Uganda.

Kellaghan, T., & Greaney, V. (1992). Using examination to improve education: A study in fourteen African countries. Washington: The World Bank.

Kellaghan, T., & Greaney, V. (2001). Using assessment to improve the quality of education. Paris: UNESCO/IIEP.

Kim, G.-J. (2001, Dec.). Education policies and reform in South Korea. Paper presented at the Secondary education in Africa: strategies for renewal, UNESCO/BREDA-World Bank Regional Workshop.

Koruna, S., & Luggen, M. (2003). Can core competences be planned? A theoretical model for core competence planning. Zurich: Technology and Innovation Management: ETH-Center for Enterprise Science Swiss Federal Institute of Technology.

Kuhn, T. S. (1996). The structure of scientific revolutions (3rd ed.). Chicago: The University of Chicago Press.

Kulpoo, D. (1998). The quality of education: some policy suggestions based on a survey of schools. Mauritius. (SACMEQ Policy Research: Report No. 1). Paris, France: UNESCO/IIEP.

Lam, Y. R., Wong, K.-C., & Ho, L.-m. (2002). School effectiveness of a streamed-school system: A multilevel modeling of the Hong Kong secondary schools. Australian Journal of Education, 46(3), 287-304.

Lance, K. C. (2002, June). What research tell us about the importance of school libraries. Paper presented at the White House Conference on School Libraries, White House.

Lassibille, G., & Tan, J. P. (2001). Are private schools more efficient than public schools? Evidence from Tanzania. Education Economics, 9(2), 145-172.

Lassibille, G., Tan, J. P., & Sumra, S. (1998). Expansion of private secondary education: Experience and prospects in Tanzania (Working Paper No. 12). Washington D.C.: Development Research Group. The World Bank.

Lassibille, G., Tan, J. P., & Sumra, S. (2000). Expansion of private secondary education: Lessons from recent experience in Tanzania. Comparative Education Review, 44(1), 1-28.

Lawton, D. (1994). Defining quality. In P. Ribbins & E. Burridge (Eds.), Improving education promoting quality in schools (pp. 1-7). London: Cassell.

Leaver, E. D. (2003). Do resources matter? An analysis of the effects of high school resources on the performances of students bound for selective colleges and universities, with special emphasis on students in high poverty high schools. Unpublished Dissertation, University of Notre Dame, Notre Dame, Indiana.

Lee, J. W., & Barro, R. J. (1997). Schooling quality in a cross section of countries. Cambridge, MA: National Bureau of Economic Research.

Lee, S., Brown, G., Mekis, C., & Singh, D. (2003, August 2003). Education for school librarians: Trends and issues from selected developing countries. Paper presented at the World Library and Information Congress: 69th IFLA General Conference and Council, Berlin.

Lee, V. E. (1997). Effective secondary schools. In L. J. Saha (Ed.), International Encyclopedia of the Sociology of Education (pp. 437-443). Oxford, UK: Elsevier Science Ltd.

Levacic, R., & Glover, D. (1997). Value for money as a school improvement strategy: Evidence from the new inspection system in England. School Effectiveness and School Improvement, 8(2), 231-253.

Levin, H. M. (1989). Mapping the economics of education an introductory essay. Educational Researcher, 18(4), 13-16.

Lewin, K. (2002). Options for post primary education and training in Uganda: Increasing access, equity, and effeciency. A framework for policy. Kampala: Ministry of Education and Sports.

Lewin, K. M. (2000). Mapping science education policy in developing countries.

Washington, DC: World Bank, Human Development Network Secondary Education Series.
Lewin, K. M. (2001a). Are higher secondary enrolment rates achievable? In K. M. Lewin & F. Caillods (Eds.), Financing secondary education in the developing countries: Strategies for sustainable growth (pp. 39-60). Paris: UNESCO Publishing.
Lewin, K. M. (2001b). Statement of the problem. In K. M. Lewin & F. Caillods (Eds.), Financing secondary education in developing countries: Strategies for sustainable growth (pp. 5-19). Paris: UNESCO Publishing.

Lewin, K. M. (2001c). The status of secondary schooling in developing countries. In K. M. Lewin & F. Caillods (Eds.), Financing secondary education in developing countries: Strategies for sustainable growth (pp. 21-37). Paris: UNESCO Publishing.
Lewin, K. M. (2002). Options for post primary education and training in Uganda: Increasing access, equity, and efficiency. A framework for policy. Kampala: Ministry of Education and Sports.
Lewin, K. M., & Caillods, F. (Eds.). (2001). Financing secondary education in developing countries: Strategies for sustainable growth. Paris: UNESCO Publishing.
Lewin, K. M., & Gunne, M. (2000). Policy and practice in assessment in Anglophone Africa: does globalization explain convergence? Assessment in Education, 7(3), 379.
Lewin, P. (2004). Firms, resources and production functions: The relevance of the new growth economics for the theory of the firm. Retrieved January 15th, 2004, from www.utdallas.edu/~plewin/
Liang, X. (2002). Uganda post-primary education sector report. Kampala, Uganda: Human Development Sector: Africa Region, The World Bank.
Little, A. (2000). Qualification, quality, and equality A political economy of Sri Lankan education 1971-1993. In A. R. Welch (Ed.), Third World Education quality of equality (pp. 201-222). New York and London: Garland Publishing, Inc.
Livingstone, D. W. (1997). The limits of human capital theory: expanding knowledge, informal learning and underemployment. Policy Options (July /August 1997), 9-13.
Lloyd, C. B., Tawila, S. E., Clark, W. H., & Mensch, B. S. (2003). The impact of educational quality on school exit in Egypt. Comparative Education Review, 47(4), 444-467.
Lockheed, M., & Hanushek, E. (1988). Improving educational effieciency in developing countries: What do we know? Compare, 18(1), 21-38.
Lockheed, M. E., & Hanushek, E. A. (1988). Improving educational efficiency in developing countries: What do we know? Compare, 18(1), 21-38.
Lockheed, M. E., & Levin, H. M. (1993). Creating effective schools. In H. M. Levin & M. E. Lockheed (Eds.), Effective schooling in developing countries (pp. 1-19). London: The Falmer Press.
Lockheed, M. E., Verspoor, A. M., Bloch, B., Englebert, P., Fuller, B., King, E., et al. (1991). Improving primary education in developing countries. Oxford: Oxford University Press (Published for the World Bank).
Lonsdale, M. (2003). Impact of school libraries on student achievement: a review

of the research. Victoria: Australian Council for Educational Research (ACER): Report for the Australian School Library Association.

Lopez-Acevedo, G., & Salinas, A. (2001). Teacher salaries and professional profile in Mexico (LCSHD Paper Series No. 63). Mimeo: The World Bank: Latin America and the Caribbean Regional Office.

Ludwig, J., & Bassi, L. J. (1999). The puzzling case of school resources and student achievement. Educational Evaluation and Policy Analysis, 21(4), 385-403.

Luxton, S., Farrelly, F., & Salmon, G. (2000). The development and delivery of an emaster of marketing TM_ A Resource Based Approach. Paper number 57. Retrieved September 26th, 2003, from http://www.com.unisa.edu.au/cccc/papers/refereed/paper57-1.htm

Lyons, J. B. (2001). Do school facilities really impact a child's education? Scottsdale, AZ: Council of Educational Facility Planners International.

Machingaidze, T., Pfukani, P., & Shumba, S. (1998). The quality of primary education: some policy suggestions based on a survey of schools. Zimbabwe. (SACMEQ Policy Research No. 3). Paris: UNESCO/IIEP.

Maijoor, S., & Witteloostuijn, A. V. (1996). An empirical test of the resource-based theory: Strategic regulation in the Dutch Audit Industry. Strategic Management Journal, 17(7), 549-569.

Makwati, G., Audinos, B., & Lairez, T. (2003). The role of statistics in improving the quality of basic education in Sub-Saharan Africa. Paper presented at the ADEA Biennial Meeting 2003, Grand, Baie, Mauritius, December 3-6.

Mann, T. (2001). The importance of books, free access, and libraries as places and the dangerous inadequacy of the information science paradigm. The Journal of Academic Librarianship, 27(4), 268-281.

Marion, R., & Flanigan, J. (2001). Evolution and punctuation of theories of educational expenditure and student outcomes. Journal of Educational Finance, 26(Winter 2001), 239-258.

Markides, C. C., & Williamson, P. J. (1996). Corporate diversification and organizational structure: A resource-based view. Academy of Management Journal, 39(2), 340-367.

Marsh, S. J., & Ranft, A. L. (1999). Why resources matter: An empirical study of the influence of knowledge-Based resources on new market entry. In M. A. Hitt, R. D. Nixon, P. G. Clifford & K. P. Coyne (Eds.), Dynamic strategic resources: Development, diffusion and integration. Chistester-New York: John Wiley & Sons ltd.

Mata, F. J., Fuerst, W. L., & Barney, J. B. (1995). Information technology and sustainable competitive advantage: A resource-based analysis. MIS Quarterly, 19(4), 487-505.

Mayeske, G. W., Okada, T., Beaton, A. E., Cohen, W., & Wisler, C. E. (1973). A study of achievement of our nation's students. Washington: U. S. Government Printing Office.

McGuffey, C. W. (1982). Facilities. In H. J. Walberg (Ed.), Improving educational standards and productivity (pp. 237-288). Berkeley, California: McCutchan Publishing Corporation.

Miles, J., & Shevlin, M. (2001). Applying regression & correlation: A guide for students and researchers. London: SAGE Publications.

Miller, D., & Shamse, J. (1996). The Resource-Based View of the firm in two environments: The Hollywood film studios from 1936 to 1965. Academy of

Management Journal, 39(3), 519-543.
Mingat, A. (2003). Analytical and factual elements for a quality policy for primary education in Sub-Saharan Africa in the context of education for all. Paper presented at the ADEA Biennial Meeting 2003, Grand Baie, Mauritius, December 3-6.
MOES. (2001). Basic requirements and minimum standards indicators for educational institutions. Kampala: Ministry of Education and Sports.
MOES. (2002). Universal primary education (UPE) Publication 2001-2002. Kampala, Uganda: Ministry of Education and Sports, Republic of Uganda.
MOES. (2004). Education profile. Retrieved April 27, 2004, from http://www.ugandainvest.com/education.pdf
Monk, D. H. (1992). Educational productivity research: An update and assessment of its role in finance reform. Educational Evaluation and Policy Analysis, 14(4), 307-332.
Monk, D. H., & Plecki, M. L. (1999). Generating and managing resources for school improvement. In J. Murphy & K. S. Louis (Eds.), Handbook of research on educational administration (2nd ed.). San Francisco: Jossey-Bass Publishers.
Mortimore, P. (1991). Effective schools from a British perspective: Research and practice. In j. R. Bliss, W. A. Firestone & C. E. Richards (Eds.), Rethinking effective schools: Research and practice (pp. 76-90). Englewood Cliffs, New jersey: Prentice Hall.
Mugimu, C. B., & Hite, S. J. (2001). Uganda needs quality educational research. The Educational Magazine Journal of Education, 3(2), 12-15.
Munro, B. H. (2001a). Regression. In B. H. Munro (Ed.), Statistical methods for health care research (4th ed., pp. 245-269). Philadelphia: Lippincott.
Munro, B. H. (2001b). Regression diagnostics and conical correlation. In B. H. Munro (Ed.), Statistical methods for health care research (4th ed., pp. 271-302). Philidelphia: Lipponcott.
Munro, B. H., Jacobsen, B. S., Duffy, M. E., & Braitman, L. E. (2001). Introduction to inferential statistics and hypothesis testing. In B. H. Munro (Ed.), Statistical methods for health care research (4th ed., pp.63-94). Philadelphia: Lippincott.
Murnane, R. J. (1981). Interpreting the evidence on school effectiveness. Teachers College Record, 83(1), 19-35.
Murphy, P. D. (2003). Uganda: Adjustment operations in support of education. Retrieved Dec. 1st, 2003, from www.sustdev.org/Features/uganda.html
Mutakyahwa, R. G. (1999). Financing, delivery and management of education services in Tanzania. In T. L. Maliyamkono & O. Ogbu (Eds.), Cost sharing in education and health (pp. 23-80). Dar es Salaam, Tanzania: Tema Publishers Company Ltd.
Myers, J. L., & Well, A. D. (2003). Research design and statistical analysis (2nd ed.). Mahwah, New Jersey: Lawrence Erlbaum Associates, Publishers.
Nassor, S., & Mohammed, K. A. (1998). The quality of education: some policy suggestions based on a survey of schools. Zanzibar (SACMEQ Policy Research No. 4). Paris: UNESCO/IIEP.
Nicholson, W. (1998). Microeconomic Theory: Basic principles and extensions (7th ed.). Fort Worth: The Dryden Press Harcourt Brace College Publishers.
Nixon, R. D., Bishop, K., Clouse, V. G. H., & Kemelgor, B. H. (2003). From experiment to entrepreneurial education: Prior knowledge and

entrepreneurial discovery. Retrieved November 18th, 2003, from http://sbaer.uca.edu/research/2003/icsb/papers/11.doc

Nkamba, M., & Kanyika, J. (1998). The quality of education: some policy suggestions based on a survey of schools. Zambia. (SACMEQ Policy Research No. 5). Paris: UNESCO/IIEP.

Nsubuga, Y. (2004). Background information. Kampala, Uganda: Ministry of Education.

Nyagura, L. M., & Riddell, A. (1993). Primary school achievement in English and Mathematics in Zimbabwe (Working papers No. WPS 1208). Washington, D. C.: The World Bank.

Odden, A., & Archibald, S. (2001). Committing to class-size reduction and finding the resources to implement it: A case study for resource reallocation. Educational Policy Analysis Archives, 9(30).

Papas, G., & Psacharopoulos, G. (1991a). The determinants of educational achievement in Greece. In A. Lewy, M. Alkin, B. McGaw & R. Langeheine (Eds.), Studies in educational evaluation. Oxford: Pergamon Press.

Papas, G., & Psacharopoulos, G. (1991b). The determinants of educational achievement in Greece. Studies in Educational Evaluation, 17(2/3), 405-418.

Penrose, E. (1959). The theory of the growth of the firm (1st ed.). New York: John Wiley & Sons, Inc.

Penrose, E. (1995). The theory of the growth of the firm (3rd ed.). Oxford: Oxford University Press.

Peteraf, M. A. (1993). The cornerstone of competitive advantage: A resource-based view. Strategic Management Journal, 14(3), 179-191.

Peteraf, M. A., & Bergen, M. E. (2003). Scanning dynamic competitive landscapes: A market-based and resource based framework. Strategic Management Journal, 24, 1027-1041.

Picus, L. O. (1997). Does money matter in education? A policy maker's guide: Selected Papers in School Finance 1995. In W. J. J. Fowler (Ed.), U. S. Department of Education. National Center for Education Statistics. Selected papers in school finance 1995, NCES 97-536 (pp. 15-36). University of Southern California.

Psacharopoulos, G. (1994). Returns to investment in education: A global update. World Development, 22, 1325-1343.

Psacharopoulos, G. (2000). Economics of education a la Euro. European Journal of Education, 35(1), 81-96.

Ralph, J. H., & Fennessey, J. (1983). "Science or reform: some questions about effective schools model". Phi Delta Kappa International, 64(10), 689-695.

Rameckers, F. J. M. A. (2001, Dec.). Effective monitoring of the quality of education: Towards a managerial and participatory approach. Paper presented at the Secondary education in Africa: Strategies for renewal, UNESCO/BREDA-World Bank Regional Workshop in Mauritius on the renewal of African secondary education.

Randall, E. V., Cooper, B. S., & Hite, S. J. (1999). Understanding the politics of research in education. In B. S. Cooper & E. V. Randall (Eds.), Accuracy or advocacy: The politics of research in education. Thousand Oaks, California: Corwin Press, Inc.

Ray, G., Barney, J. B., & Muhanna, W. A. (2004). Capabilities, business processes, and competitive advantage: Choosing the dependent variable in empirical tests of the resource-based view. Strategic Management Journal, 25, 23-37.

Reynolds, D. (1990). Research on school organizational effectiveness: The end of the beginning? In R. Saran & V. Trafford (Eds.), Research in education management and policy (pp. 9-23). London: The Falmer Press.

Reynolds, D. (1994). School effectiveness and quality in education. In P. Ribbins & E. Burridge (Eds.), Improving education promoting quality in schools (pp. 18-31). London: Cassell.

Richards, C. E. (1991a). The meaning and measure of school effectiveness. In J. R. Bliss, W. A. Firestone & C. E. Richards (Eds.), Rethinking effective schools research and practice (pp. 28-42). Englewoods Cliffs, New Jersey: Prentice Hall.

Richards, C. E. (1991b). Postscript: Rethinking effective schools. In J. R. Bliss, W. A. Firestone & C. E. Richards (Eds.), Rethinking effective schools: Research and practice (pp. 185-188). Englewood Cliffs, New Jersey: Prentice Hall.

Riddell, A. R. (1997). Assessing designs for school effectiveness research and school improvement in developing countries. Comparative Education Review, 41(2), 178-204.

Riddell, A. R., & Nyagura, L. M. (1991). What causes differences in achievement in Zimbabwe's secondary schools? (Working Papers No. WPS 705). Washington, D. C.: Population and Human Resources Department; The World Bank.

Ross, K. N., & Mahlck, L. (Eds.). (1990). Planning the quality of education: The collection and use of data for informed decision-making. Paris: Pergamon Press.

Rouse, M. J., & Daellenbach, U. S. (1999). Rethinking research methods for the resource-based perspective: Isolating sources of sustainable competitive advantage. Strategic Management Journal, 20, 487-494.

Rouse, M. J., & Daellensbach, U. S. (2002). Research notes commentaries: more thinking on research methods for the resource-based perspective. Strategic Management Journal, 23, 963-967.

Rugman, A. M., & Verbeke, A. (2002). Edith Penrose's contribution to the resource-based view of strategic management. Strategic Management Journal, 23, 769-780.

Rumelt, R. P. (1984). Towards a strategic theory of the firm. In R. B. Lamb (Ed.), Competitive strategic management (pp. 556-570). Englewood Cliffs, New Jersey: Prince-Hall, Inc.

Rumelt, R. P. (1991). How much does industry matter? Strategic Management Journal, 12(3), 167-185.

Rutter, M. (1980). Secondary-school practice and pupil success. In M. Marland (Ed.), Education for the inner city (pp. 125-146). London: Heinemann Educational Books.

Rutter, M. (1983). School effects on pupil progress: Research findings and policy implications. Child Development, 54(1), 1-29.

Rutter, M., Maughan, B., Mortimore, P., Ouston, J., & Smith, A. (1979). Fifteen thousand hours: Secondary schools and their effects on children. Cambridge, Massachusetts: Harvard University Press.

Sanders, N. M. (2002a). Would privatization of K-12 schooling lead to competition and thereby improve education? An industrial organization aanlysis.

References

Educational policy analysis achieves(May 2002), 264-287.

Sanders, N. M. (2002b). Would privatization of K-12 schooling lead to competition and thereby improve education? An industrial organization analysis. Educational Policy Analysis Archives, 264-287.

Scheerens, J. (1991). Process indicators of school functioning: A selection based on the research literature on school effectiveness. Studies in Educational Evaluation, 17(2/3), 371-403.

Scheerens, J. (1992). Process indicators of school functioning. In N. Bottani & H. J. Walberg (Eds.), The OECD international education indicators: A framework for analysis (pp. 53-76). Paris: OECD Publications.

Scheerens, J. (1999). School effectiveness in developed and developing countries: A review of the research evidence. Retrieved March 8th, 2003, from http://www.worldbank.org/education

Scheerens, J. (2000). Improving school effectiveness (Vol. 68). Paris: UNESCO/ IIEP.

Scheerens, J. (2001a). Introduction: School effectiveness in developing countries. School Effectiveness and School Improvement, 12(4), 353-358.

Scheerens, J. (2001b). Monitoring school effectiveness in developing countries. School Effectiveness and School Improvement, 12(4), 359-384.

Scheerens, J. (2002). School effectiveness in developed and developing countries: A review of the research evidence. Retrieved March 8th, 2003, from http://www.worldbank.org/education

Scheerens, J., & Bosker, R. J. (1997). The foundations of educational effectiveness. Oxford, UK: Elsevier Science Ltd.

Schubert, J. G., & Prouty-Harris, D. (2003). Accelerating paths to quality: A multi-faceted reality. Paper presented at the Association for the Development of Education in Africa ADEA Biennial Meeting 2003, Grand Baie, Mauritius, December 3-6, 2003.

Schultz, T. W. (1993). The economic importance of human capital in modernization. Education Economics, 1(1), 13-19.

Senge, P. M. (1990). The leader's new work: Building learning organizations. Sloan Management Review(Fall 1990), 7-23.

Senge, P. M., Kleiner, A., Roberts, C., Ross, R. B., & Smith, B. J. (1994). The fifth discipline fieldbook: Strategies and tools for building a learning organization. New York: Bantam Doubleday Dell Publishing Group, Inc.

Sergiovanni, T. L. (1984). Leadership and excellence in schooling. Educational Leadership, 41(5), 4-13.

Serrant, T. D., & McClure, M. W. (2003). Secondary education reform: Policy briefing paper. Retrieved Nov. 30th, 2003, from www.seryp.org/review/wb.html

Shive, J. A. (2000). Multilevel panel analysis of the effect of school resources on student outcomes. Unpublished Dissertation, Vanderbelt University, Navhville, Tennessee.

Silins, H. C., & Murray-Harvey, R. (1999). What makes a good senior secondary school? Journal of Educational Administration, 37(4), 329-344.

Sirkin, R. M. (1995). Statistics for the social sciences. Thousand Oaks: SAGE Publications.

Spady, W. G. (1976). The impact of school resources on students. In W. H. Sewell, R. M. Hauser & D. L. Featherman (Eds.), Schooling and achievement in American Society (pp. 185-223). New York: Academic Press.

Spencer, B. D., & Wiley, D. E. (1981). The sense and the nonsense of school effectiveness. Journal of Policy Analysis and Management, 1(1), 43-52.

Stuart, N. (1994). Quality in education. In P. Ribbins & E. Burridge (Eds.), Improving education: Promoting quality in schools (pp. 8-17). London: Cassell.

Suter, L. E. (2000). Is student achievement immutable? Evidence from international studies on schooling and student achievement. Review of Educational Research, 70(4), 529-545.

Tamukong, J. A. (1997). Strategies to mobilize local resources to finance secondary school education in the north west province of Cameroon. Canadian and International Education, 26(2), 81-86.

Taylor, B. M., Pearson, P. D., Clark, K., & Walpole, S. (2000). Effective schools and accomplished teachers: Lessons about primary-grade reading instruction in low-income schools. The Elementary School Journal, 101(2), 121-165.

Teddlie, C. (2003). Case studies of school improvement in East Africa: A new addition to school effectiveness research. School Effectiveness and School Improvement, 14(2), 233-245.

Teece, D. J., Pisano, G., & Shuen, A. (1990). Firm capabilities, resources, and the concept of strategy: Four paradigms of strategic management. Berkeley, California: University of California.

Thias, H. H., & Carnoy, M. (1972). Cost-benefit analysis in education A case study of Kenya. Baltimore and London: The Johns Hopkins Press.

Thulstrup, E. W. (1999). School laboratories in developing countries are they worth the effort and expense? In S. A. Ware (Ed.), Science and environment education views from developing countries (pp. 113-128). Washington, DC: The World Bank.

Tilak, J. B. G. (1992). Public and private sectors in education in India. In R. F. Arnove, P. G. Altbach & G. P. Kelly (Eds.), Emergent issues in education: Comparative perspectives (pp. 173-185). New York: State University of New York Press.

Tomasevski, K. (1999). Economic, social and cultural rights: Addendum Mission to Uganda 26th June- 2 July 1999. Kampala, Uganda: Commission on Human Rights.

Tooley, J. (2000). The private sector serving the educational needs of the poor: A case study from India with policy recommendations. Paper presented at the Pubic-Private Partnerships in Education Program, Tokyo 29 May - 7 June 2000.

Tooley, J. (2001). Serving the needs of the poor: The private education sector in developing countries. In C. R. Hepburn (Ed.), Can market save our schools? (pp. 167-184). Vancouver, British Colombia: The Fraser Institute.

Tooley, J. (2002). Private education: What the poor can teach us. Policy, 18(1), 19-21.

Tooley, J. (2003, January 18th, 2003). A lesson from the third World: James Tooley on the extraordinary success of private education in Africa and India. Retrieved September 5th,, 2003, from www.spectator.co.uk/article

Tooley, J., Dixon, P., & Stanfield, L. (2003). Delivering better education: Market solutions for educational improvement. England: ASI (Research) Ltd 2003.

References

Townsend, T. (1997). What makes schools effective? A comparison between school communities in Australia and USA*. School Effectiveness and School Improvement, 8(3), 311-326.

Tsang, M. C. (2002). Comparing the costs of public and private schools in developing countries. In H. M. Levin & P. J. McEwan (Eds.), Cost-Effectiveness and educational policy (pp. 111-136). Larchmont, NY: Eye on Education, Inc.

UNDP. (2002). East Timor: The way ahead. National Human Development Report 2002. The education horizon. Retrieved October 8th,, 2002

UNESCO. (1994). World declaration on education for all and framework for action to meet basic learning needs. Jomtien, Thailand 5-6 March 1990: UNESCO.

UNESCO. (1997). Report on the state of education in Africa: Challenges and reconstruction. Dakar, Senegal: UNESCO Regional Office for Education in Africa (BREDA).

UNESCO. (2001). IIEP's Programmes Medium-Term Plan 2002-2007. Retrieved February 4th, 2003, from http://www.unesco.org/iiep

UNESCO. (2003a). High-level Group on Education for All second meeting Report 2002. Abuja, Nigeria: UNESCO.

UNESCO. (2003b, October 3-4). Ministerial Round Table "On Quality Education". Paper presented at the General Conference 32nd Session, UNESCO Headquarters, Paris.

Velez, E., Schiefelbein, E., & Valenzuela, J. (1993). Factors affecting achievement in primary education (Working paper No. HROWP2). Washington D. C.: The World Bank, Human Resources Development and Operations Policy.

Venkatraman, N., & Ramanujam, V. (1986). Measuring of business performance in strategy research: A comparison of approaches. The Academy of Management Review, 11(4), 801-814.

Voigts, F. (1998). The quality of education: Some policy suggestions based on a survey of schools. Namibia. (SACMEQ Policy Research No. 2). Paris.

Ware, S. A. (1992a). The education of secondary science teachers in developing countries. Washington, D. C.: World Bank.

Ware, S. A. (1992b). Secondary school science in developing countries (PHREE Background Paper No. 92/53). Washington, D.C.: World Bank.

Ware, S. A. (Ed.). (1999). Science and environmental education views from developing countries. Washington, DC.: The World Bank.

Warwick, D. P., & Jatoi, H. (1994). Teacher gender and student achievement in Pakistan. Comparative Education Review, 38(3), 377-400.

Watkins, K., Watt, P., & Buston, O. (2001). Education charges: A tax on human development (Oxfam Briefing Paper). London, Great Britain: Oxfam International.

Wayne, A. J., & Youngs, P. (2003). Teacher characteristics and student achievement gains: A review. Review of Educational Research, 73(1), 89-122.

Welch, A. R. (2000). Quality and equality in third world education. In A. R. Welch (Ed.), Third world education; equality and equity (pp. 3-28). New York: Garland Publishing.

Werf, G. V. d., Creemers, B., & Guldemond, H. (2001). Improving parental involvement in primary education in Indonesia: Implementation, effects and costs. School Effectiveness and School Improvement, 12(4), 477-466.

Wernerfelt, B. (1984). A resource-Based View of the firm. Strategic Management Journal, 5(2), 171-180.
Wernerfelt, B. (1995). The resource-based view of the firm: Ten years after. Strategic Management Journal, 16, 171-174.
Wernerfelt, B., & Montgomery, C. A. (1988). Tohin'sq and the importance of focus in firm performance. The American Economic Review, 78(1), 246-250.
Williams, D., Coles, L., & Wavell, C. (2002). Impact of school library services on achievement and learning in primary schools. London, UK: Department of Education & Skills and Resource: The Council for Museums. Archives & Libraries.
Willms, J. D., & Somers, M.-A. (2001). Family, classroom, and school effects on children's educational outcomes in Latin America. School Effectiveness and School Improvement, 12(4), 409-445.
Wobmann, L. (2000). Schooling resources, educational institutions, and student performance: The international evidence (Working Paper No. 983). Kiel, Germany: Kiel Institute of World Economics.
Wobmann, L. (2001). New evidence on the missing resource-performance link in education (Kiel Working Paper No. 1051). Kiel, Germany: Kiel Institute of World Economics.
Wobmann, L. (2003). How does East Asia achieve its high educational performance? Kiel, Germany: Kiel Institute for World Economics.
Wobmann, L., & West, M. R. (2002). Class-size effects in school systems around the world: Evidence from between-grade variation in TIMSS (Kiel Working Paper No. 1099). Kiel, Germany: Kiel Institute for World Economics.
Woessmann, L. (2001). Why students in some countries do better: International evidence on the importance of education policy. Education Matters, 1(2), 67-74.
WorldBank. (1994). Educational quality: defining what's important (No. 16). Washington D. C.: Africa Technical Department: The World Bank Group.
WorldBank. (1995). Development in progress: Priorities and strategies for education a World review (2nd ed.). Washington DC: World Bank Publication
WorldBank. (2001). Education for dynamic economies: Accelerating progress towards education for all (AFA) (Working Paper No. DC2001-0025). Washington D.C.: The World Bank.
WorldBank. (2002). Achieving universal primary education in Uganda: The "Big Bang" approach (Human Development Network education notes). Washington, D. C.: Human Development Network: The World Bank.
WorldBank. (2003). World Development Indicators. Washington, DC: International Bank.
Worthen, B. R., White, K. R., Fan, X., & Sudweeks, R. R. (1999). Measurement and assessment in schools (2nd ed.). Don Mills, Ontorio: Longman.
Wyatt, T. (1996). School effectiveness research: Dead end, damp squib or smouldering fuse? Issues in Educational Research, 6(1), 79-112.
Yeom, M., & McClure, M. W. (2001, 30 April 2001). Secondary education reform: Policy briefing paper. Retrieved Nov. 30th, 2003, from
Young, M. D. (1999). Multifocal educational policy research: toward a method for enhancing traditional educational policy studies. American Educational Research Journal, 36(4), 677-714.

References

Young, P. V. (2000). Scientific social surveys and research (4th ed.). New Delhi: Prentice-Hall of India.

Yudof, M., Levin, B., Moran, R., & Kirp, D. L. (2002). Educational policy and the law (Fourth ed.). Belmont, CA: Wadsworth.

APPENDIX A: SUMMARY OF RBV EMPIRICAL STUDIES

Author(s)	Methodology	Construct(s) or attribute(s)	Result & Statistic techniques
Wernerfelt & Montgomery 1988	Tobin's q (capital market value of the firm divided by the replacement value of its assets)	Ind. Varia.: Focus, industry, and share effects Dep. Varia.: firm performance	Regressions and partial correlation, least squares estimation, Adjusted Rsqs.
Durand (1999)	Qualitative techniques face-to-face interviews with CEOs	Inde. Varia.: Inimitability of productive resources, non-transferability of productive resources, Non-Substitutability of suppliers relationships, Non-substitutability of customer relationships, and Internal coordination Dep. Varia.: Returns on sales, assets, & market performance	Descriptive statistics, the correlation matrix, LISREL for principal component analysis, multiple correlation
Marsh & Renet (1999)	Survey techniques	Inde. Varia.: Relateness, Tacitness & embeddedness, uncertainity, Dep. Varia.: performance	Linear regression & Multinomial logistic regression analysis, Pearson correlation, descriptive statistics,
Barney & Wright (1998)		Valueness, rareness, imitability, & organization	VRIO framework
Luxton, etal 2000		Value, barrier of duplication	
Nixon et	Experimental	Value, rarity, imperfect	Descriptive statistics

Appendices

APPENDIX B

SECONDARY SCHOOL SITE SURVEY - 2003

Personnel Survey (PART 1)

Administrator, Teacher and Staff Resources

We appreciate your willingness to participate with Brigham Young University (U.S.A.) in conducting research addressing the role of resources in secondary schools in Uganda.

This School Site Survey is composed of three parts: PART 1: Consent Form and Personnel Survey

PART 2: Headmaster Survey

PART 3: Deputy Headmaster Survey

We would appreciate your help in completing PART 1 of this survey either before or after our scheduled appointment.

SCHOOL INFORMATION: Please print your name and information about your school:

School Name: _____
Interviewee Name: _____
Post: _____

ADMINISTRATOR RESOURCES: Please tell us about the administrators at your school:

1. _____ How many administrators live at the school or have their accommodation funded by the school?
2. What is the average salary (including all wages and allowances) for your administrators per month (UGS 000's)?

       a. Below UGS 100
       b. Between UGS 101-200
       c. Between UGS 201-300
       d. Between UGS 301-400
       e. Between UGS 401-500
       f. Between UGS 501-600
       g. Between UGS 601-700
       h. Between UGS 701-800
       i. Between UGS 801-900
       j. Between UGS 901-1,000
       k. Above UGS 1,000 (one million)

3. Please list and describe your administrators:

	Administrator by first name	Title	Gender? M/F	Full/part time? F/P	Age Range: 1=20-30 2=31-40 3=41-50 4=51-60 5=Over 60	Total # of years at school?	# Years Admin experience at another school?	# of complete years of University?	Teaching or Admin Degree or Cert? Y/N	Participates in District Association?	Participates in District training?
Ex.	Frank	Clerk	M	F	2	4	2	4	Y	Y	Y
1											
2											
3											
4											
5											
6											
7											
8											
9											
10											
11											
12											
13											
14											
15											

STAFF RESOURCES: Please tell us about your school's staff members (all functions except administrators and teachers).

4. _____ How many staff are employed by the school (not administrators or teachers)?
5. _____ How many full time staff members work at the school?
6. _____ How many part time staff members work at the school?
7. _____ How many staff members live at the school?
8. _____ How many staff members live elsewhere and have accommodation funded by the school?
9. _____ How many male staff members work at the school?
10. _____ How many female staff members work at the school?
11. What is the average salary for your staff members per month (in UGS 1,000's)?
        a. Below UGS 50
        b. Between UGS 51-100
        c. Between UGS 101-150
        d. Between UGS 151-200
        e. Over UGS 200

Appendices

TEACHER RESOURCES: Please tell us about your teachers.

12. ____ How many teachers live off-campus and have accommodation funded by the school?
13. ____ How many of your teachers that live on campus also teach at other schools?
14. ____ How many of your teachers live at other schools yet teach subjects at your school?
15. ____ How many of your teachers are NOT certified?
16. ____ How many of the teachers also perform administrative duties?
17. ____ How many department heads do you have?
18. YES   NO   Are department heads paid extra?
19. How much extra money (UGS) are department heads paid?
    _____UGS per _____ (specify month, term, etc.)
20. _____ How many teachers left (stopped teaching at) your school last year?
21. Of those teachers that left, how many found employment in the following sectors:
    a. __ Private Schools   b. __ Government Schools   c. __ Private Sector
    d.__ Other

22. For which subjects are teachers the hardest to find (list)? _____
    _____

23. Which subjects lose teachers the most (list)? _____
    _____

24. In this past year, have you paid your teachers' salaries:
    a. __ Almost always late   b. __ Sometimes late   c. __ Usually on time
    d.__ Always on time
25. How much control do teachers generally have over instructional materials, curriculum and class time?
    a. __ Very little control   b. __ Some control   c.__ Quite a bit of control
    d.__ Total control
26. ____ How many of the teachers are examiners for UNEB exams?
27. ____ How many of the teachers are markers for the UNEB exams?
28. ____ How many examiners do you contract to help your candidates?
    How often? _____
29. ____ How many markers do you contract to mark your exams?
30. What is the average salary for your teachers per month (in UGS 1,000's)?
    a. Below UGS 100
    b. Between UGS 101-200
    c. Between UGS 201-300
    d. Between UGS 301-400
    e. Between UGS 401-500
    f. Above UGS 500

31. ____ What is the average number of different subjects for each teacher?
32. ____ Lowest number for a teacher?   ____ Highest number for a teacher?

School Resources and Performance in Developing Countries

33. Please describe the total number of teachers at your school (during the last term):
    Subjects: M=Math   H=History   E=English   B=Biology   C=Chemistry
                G=Geography   W=Computers   O=Other

#	Teacher by first name	Main Subjects (write in):	Full or part time? F/P	Gender? M/F	Age Range: 1=20-30 2=31-40 3=41-50 4=51-60	# yrs at school	Lives at your school?	# of subjects taught	Teach elsewhere?	Finding a replacement for this teacher would be: 1=Fairly easy 2=Somewhat difficult 3=Very difficult
Ex.	Frank	Math and Science	F	M	2	3	Y	2	Y	2
1										
2										
3										
4										
5										
6										
7										
8										
9										
10										
11										
12										
13										
14										
15										
16										
17										

Appendices

#	Teacher by first name	Main Subjects (write in):	Full or part time? F/P	Gender? M/F	Age Range: 1=20-30 2=31-40 3=41-50 4=51-60	# yrs at school	Lives at your school?	# of subjects taught	Teach elsewhere?	Finding a replacement for this teacher would be: 1=Fairly easy 2=Somewhat difficult 3=Very difficult
Ex.	Frank	Math and Science	F	M	2	3	Y	2	Y	2
19										
20										
21										
22										
23										
24										
25										
26										
27										
28										
29										
30										
31										
32										
33										
34										
35										
36										
37										
38										
39										
40										
41										
42										
43										
44										
45										
46										
47										

School Resources and Performance in Developing Countries

#	Teacher by first name	Main Subjects (write in):	Full or part time? F/P	Gender? M/F	Age Range: 1=20-30 2=31-40 3=41-50 4=51-60	# yrs at school	Lives at your school?	# of subjects taught	Teach elsewhere?	Finding a replacement for this teacher would be: 1=Fairly easy 2=Somewhat difficult 3=Very difficult
Ex.	Frank	Math and Science	F	M	2	3	Y	2	Y	2
49										
50										
51										
52										
53										
54										
55										
56										
57										
58										
59										
60										
61										
62										
63										
64										
65										
66										
67										
68										
69										
70										
71										
72										
73										
74										
75										

Appendices

TEACHING RESOURCES: Please describe the resources you have for teaching.

34. Please describe the more permanent teaching resources in your school.

Teaching Resources (These resources are reusable.) (Add additional teaching resources if they are not listed)	Number (count)	Overall Condition 1 = Poor 2 = Fair 3 = Good 4 = Very Good 5 = Excellent	How expensive is this resource? 1 = Not expensive 2 = Slightly 3 = Somewhat 4 = Very 5 = Extremely	How important is this resource? 1 = Not important 2 = Slightly 3 = Somewhat 4 = Very 5 = Extremely
Chalkboards				
Maps				
Wall charts				
Tables				
Student Desks (1 person)				
Student Desks (3 person)				
Textbooks				
Math				
English				
Geography				
Biology				
History				
Chemistry				
Laboratory Equipment				
Beakers				
Bunsen Burner				
Microscope				
Test Tubes				
Tripod Stands				
Conical Flasks				
Litmus Paper				
Masses				

School Resources and Performance in Developing Countries

APPENDIX B (CONTINUED)

SECONDARY SCHOOL SITE SURVEY - 2003

Headmaster Survey (PART 2)

Financial and Administrative Resources

We appreciate your willingness to participate with Brigham Young University (U.S.A.) in conducting research addressing the role of resources in secondary schools in Uganda.

This School Site Survey is composed of three parts:
PART 1: Consent Form and Personnel Survey
PART 2: Headmaster Survey
PART 3: Deputy Headmaster Survey

We would appreciate your help and guidance in completing each of the three parts. As you are the Headmaster, we would be grateful if you would complete PART 1 before or after our scheduled appointment.

We would also appreciate being able to work with you and your Deputy Headmaster to complete PARTS 2 and 3 during our scheduled visit. If you would prefer to complete the entire survey yourself (PARTS 1-3), that would be fine. However, we are aware of your many important duties and may be able to obtain this information from your associates under your direction.
Before beginning the survey, please review PARTS 2 and 3, and determine how you would prefer to complete each part. If there are several researchers on site today, and if you so direct, they may be able to work with your Deputy Headmaster or additional school administrators to complete PARTS 2 and 3.

SCHOOL INFORMATION: Please print your name and information about your school:

Interviewee's Name: _____
Post: _____
School: _____
Phone #: _____
Town/Trading Center/Village: _____
Year School Started: _____
School License #: _____
Registration #: _____
UNEB #: _____ 1st Year of UNEB: _____
Mailing Address: _____
School Founder: SELF or _____
(circle)   or   (print name)

HEADMASTER: Please tell us about yourself:

1.   In what year were you born?

2.   Female   Male   Gender (please circle)

Appendices

3.   What is your university degree?
Type: _____

Field: _____

University: _____

Date of Completion: _____

4. _____How many total years have you been in your current administrative post?
5. _____How many total years have you worked as an administrator?
6. _____How many total years have you taught in schools?
7. _____In how many different schools have you worked (total for both teaching and administration)?
8. YES NO Are you a member of the Mukono Headmaster and Teacher Association?

STUDENT COMPOSITION: Please tell us about your students:

9. _____ What is your total student enrollment? Of these students, how many are:
   ____ Girls? _____ Boys?
   ____ Boarding students? _____ Day students?
10. _____ How many new students applied to your school last year?
11. _____ How many total new students did you accept last year?
12. How many new students did you accept into each form this last year?
   S1 _____ S2 _____ S3 _____ S4 _____ S5 _____ S6 _____
13. What percentage of your students are from village areas?
   __ 0-25% __ 26-50% __ 51-75% __ 76-100%
15. What percentage of your students are from urban areas?
   __ 0-25% __ 26-50% __ 51-75% __ 76-100%
16. What percentage of students are from low-income families?
   __ 0-25% __ 26-50% __ 51-75% __ 76-100%
17. What percentage of students are from middle-income families?
   __ 0-25% __ 26-50% __ 51-75% __ 76-100%
18. What percentage of students are from high-income families?
   __ 0-25% __ 26-50% __ 51-75% __ 76-100%
19. _____ What is the total enrollment of non-Ugandan students attending your school?
20. _____ How many different countries do your students come from (other than Uganda)?
    a. Please list the countries: _____
21. Estimate your total student population in the following school years:
   _____ 2000-2001 _____ 2001-2002 _____ 2002-2003.

22. _____ How many students left your school after finishing O-level exams last year?
23. How many O-level students left your school last year due to drop out or transfer?
    a. For what reasons did O-level students leave your school last year (before completing exams)?
24. _____ How many students left your school after finishing A-level exams last year?
25. How many A-level students left your school last year due to drop out or transfer?
    a. For what reasons did A-level students leave your school last year (before completing exams)

26. **Tell us about seating students for national exams LAST YEAR:**

	O-Level	A-Level
How many of your own students did your school seat for national exams last year?		
How many students from other schools did your school seat for national exams last year?		
How many students did you send to another school to sit for national exams last year?		

SCHOOL SERVICES, APPLICATIONS & FEES: Please tell us about your fees:

27. If you have different fees for students, please indicate fees in the table below:

Class	Day			Boarding		
	# of Students	Fees per Term	# students on any scholarship	# of Students	Fees per Term	# students on any scholarship
S-I						
S-II						
S-III						
S-IV						
S-V						
S-VI						

28. _____ How many students paid full school fees in cash (including checks)?

Appendices

29. _____ How many students supplemented or paid part of their school fees with in-kind labor or services?

30. _____ How many students paid school fees only with in-kind labor or services?

31. For students that pay part or all of their school fees with in-kind labor or services, how do you determine the value of labor or service in exchange for school fees?

ADMINISTRATIVE RESOURCES: Please tell us about your administrative resources:

32. _____ How many administrative office rooms does your school have?
33. _____ How many administrative desks does your school have?
34. _____ How many functioning administrative typewriters does your school have?
35. _____ How many functioning photocopy machines does your school have?
36. _____ How many functioning computers are in the administrative offices? (If they do not have computers, go to question 41.)
37. _____ How many administrators use or know how to use computers?
38. YES NO   Is the computer in a room that can be locked for security?
39. How many of these functioning computers were manufactured in the following time periods:
    _____ Pre 1995   _____ 1995-1999   _____ 2000-present

40. How many of these functioning computers for administrators have the following:
    _____ 3 ½" drives
    _____ Zip drives
    _____ CD drives
    _____ CD Burning Capability
    _____ Internet connection
    _____ Connected to working printer

41. How many of these functioning computers for administrators have the following software functions:
    _____ Word Processing
    _____ Spreadsheet
    _____ Presentations or Slide Shows
    _____ Database
    _____ Games

FINANCIAL RESOURCES: Please describe your financial resources as of June 30, 2003:

42. Please estimate the amount of TOTAL financial resources your school received last year (2002-2003) from all sources combined (circle one):

a. None
b. Less than UGS 25 million
c. Between UGS 25-50 million
d. Between UGS 50-75 million
e. Between UGS 75-100 million
f. Between UGS 100-200 million
g. Between UGS 201-300 million
h. Between UGS 301-400 million
i. Between UGS 401-500 million
j. Between UGS 501-600 million
k. Between UGS 601-700 million
l. Between UGS 701-800 million
m. Between UGS 801-900 million
n. Between UGS 901-999 million
o. More than UGS 1 billion

43. Please describe the source of your school's financial resources last year. Please estimate in millions.

Source of Funding	Estimated the value received in UGS millions (last year, 2002⁄2003)
School Fees (cash)	
School Fees (in-kind)	
NGO Sources	
Government Sources - Capitation Grants	
Religious/Church Affiliation Sources	
Community Sources	
Students' Family Sources	
Other Donations (cash)	
Other Donations (in-kind)	
Gov't Capital Development Grants	
Gov't Bursary Scheme (Scholarships)	
TOTAL	

44. Please estimate the TOTAL value of your school's financial resources as of 30 June 2003 (circle one):

a. None
b. Less than UGS 25 million
c. Between UGS 25-50 million
d. Between UGS 50-75 million
e. Between UGS 75-100 million
f. Between UGS 100-200 million
g. Between UGS 201-300 million
h. Between UGS 301-400 million
i. Between UGS 400-500 million
j. Between UGS 501-600 million
k. Between UGS 601-700 million
l. Between UGS 701-800 million
m. Between UGS 801-900 million
n. Between UGS 901-999 million
o. More than UGS 1 billion

45. Please describe the composition of these financial resources by estimating, in millions, the value of each of the following financial resources as of June 2003.

Location of Financial Resources	Estimated Value in millions (as of 30 June 2003)
Bank Account (checking or savings)	
Other Cash Resources	
Resources, things or money that other people owe you	
Other:	
TOTAL	

46. Please estimate the value of your school's TOTAL non-financial assets as of 30 June 2003 (circle one):

a. None
b. Less than UGS 25 million
c. Between UGS 25-50 million
d. Between UGS 50-75 million
e. Between UGS 75-100 million
f. Between UGS 100-200 million
g. Between UGS 201-300 million
h. Between UGS 301-400 million
i. Between UGS 400-500 million
j. Between UGS 501-600 million
k. Between UGS 601-700 million
l. Between UGS 701-800 million
m. Between UGS 801-900 million
n. Between UGS 901-999 million
o. More than UGS 1 billion

Appendices

47. Please estimate the value of the school's non-cash resources.

Non- Financial Resources	Estimated Value in millions (as of 30 June 2003)
School Land	
School Vehicles	
School Computers, Furniture & Equipment	
School Inventories & Supplies	
School Building Blocks	
School Animals	
TOTAL	

48. YES   NO   Did your school receive financial assistance from donors last year?
(If no, go to question 52.)

49. _____ Approximately how many total donors contributed to your school last year (not including students' fees or in-kind payments)?

50. Please estimate the TOTAL value of future donations already promised or committed for your school next year – from all combined sources:

a. None
b. Less than   UGS   25 million
c. Between   UGS   25-50 million
d. Between   UGS   50-75 million
e. Between   UGS   75-100 million
f. Between   UGS   100-200 million
g. Between   UGS   201-300 million
h. Between   UGS   301-400 million
i. Between   UGS   400-500 million
j. Between   UGS   501-600 million
k. Between   UGS   601-700 million
l. Between   UGS   701-800 million
m. Between   UGS   801-900 million
n. Between   UGS   901-999 million
o. More than UGS   1 billion

51. Please rank up to four of the following as sources of past donations, from 1 to 4 "1" = Most Valuable; "4" = Less Valuable. Source:

a. _____ Community
b. _____ Religious or Church Organizations
c. _____ NGOs Organizations
d. _____ Students' Families
e. _____ Government Sources
f. _____ Friends of Administrators & Teachers
g. _____ Other Organizations within Uganda
h. _____ Other Organizations outside of Uganda

52. Please rank up to four the following as potential sources of future donations, from 1 to 4 ("1" = Most Valuable; "4" = Less Valuable). Source:

a. _____ Community
b. _____ Religious or Church Organizations
c. _____ NGOs Organizations
d. _____ Students' Families
e. _____ Government Sources
f. _____ Friends of Administrators & Teachers
g. _____ Other Organizations within Uganda
h. _____ Other Organizations outside of Uganda

53. YES NO Did you file revenue reports last year with government, district or town assessors?

54. YES NO Does your school have past or current financial loans? (If no, go to question 59.)

55. Please estimate the TOTAL value of your school's past financial loans cumulative up to 30 June 2003.

56. That is, how much have you borrowed since the school started AND fully repaid (circle one):

a. Less than UGS 50 million
b. Between UGS 51-250 million
c. Between UGS 251- 500 million
d. Between UGS 501-750 million
e. Between UGS 751 million -1 billion
f. More than UGS Over 1 billion

Appendices

57. Please describe the sources of these past financial loans (where you borrowed money or credit).

Financial Loan Surces	Estimated Cumulative Value in millions (Cumulative up to 30 June 2003)
Banking Institution	
Friend	
Family	
Other Schools	
Community Association	
Other:	
TOTAL	

58. Please estimate the TOTAL value of your school's current financial loans as of 30 June 2003. That is, how much have you borrowed that had not yet been repaid as of 30 June 2003 (circle one):

a. Less than UGS 50 million
b. Between UGS 51-250 million
c. Between UGS 251- 500 million
d. Between UGS 501-750 million
e. Between UGS 751 million -1 billion
f. More than UGS Over 1 billion

59. Please describe the sources of these current financial loans (where you borrowed money or credit).

Financial Loan Sources	Estimated Value in millions (as of 30 June 2003)
Banking Instituti on	
Friend	
Family	
Other Schools	
Community Association	
Other:	
TOTAL	

60. SKIP THIS QUESTION! For later: Calculate the value of school's buildings & facilities using the Deputy Headmaster Survey and the Evaluation formulas from Uganda:_____
_____

Appendices

OVERALL RESOURCES:

61. Please describe your resources using the following questions and scale:

	SCALE:				
	1	2	3	4	5
	Not	Sometimes not	Somewhat	Usually	Always

Resources	To what extent do you need more of this resource?	To what extent is this resource expensive?	How common is it for your school to share this resource with another school?	To what extent is this resource important to your school's successful performance?
Land				
Buildings				
Classrooms				
Vehicles				
Teaching Materials				
Textbooks				
Science equipment				
Science chemicals				
Food				
Water				
Electricity				
Repairs & Maintenance				

62. Which expenses took the largest proportion of your budget last year? Rank up to the top five (1 = Most, 5 = Least).

a. _____ Land
b. _____ Classrooms
c. _____ Vehicles
d. _____ Teaching Materials
e. _____ Food
f. _____ Water
g. _____ Electricity
h. _____ Teachers
i. _____ Staff
j. _____ Administrators
k. _____ Exam Seats

School Resources and Performance in Developing Countries

1. _____   Other: (Rank only if identified) _____
   _____

PARENT/SCHOOL BOARD RESOURCES:

63. _____ Approximately how many parents/guardians are actively involved in school activities?

64. YES NO   Do you have an active PTA in your school (circle)?
    If YES, about how many parents/guardians are involved? _____

65. Please describe what types of activities parents/guardians are generally involved in (list):
    _____

66. YES NO   Is the headmaster an owner of the school?

67. YES NO   Does the school have a school board?

68. _____ How many people serve on the School Board of Directors (or its equivalent)?

69. _____ How many of these people on the Board are employed at the school (as opposed to having their main employment elsewhere)?

70.   Please tell us about your streams by class and subject:

						S1-S4								
Subject	# Streams				Average Stream Size (number of students)				# of Teachers				How many of these teachers are certified in the Subject			
Class ?	1	2	3	4	1	2	3	4	1	2	3	4	1	2	3	4
Math																
Geography																
Biology																
History																
English																

71. Please indicate your average stream size (number of students) & number of teachers (by subject):

	S5-S6							
Subject	**# Streams**		**Average Stream Size (number of students)**		**# of Teachers**		**How many of these teachers are certified in the Subject**	
	5	6	5	6	5	6	5	6
Math								
Biology								
Chemistry								
Physics								
Agriculture								
Geography								
History								
English Literature								
Economics								
Divinity								
Fine Arts								
Home Economics								
General Paper								

School Resources and Performance in Developing Countries

APPENDIX B (CONTINUED)

SECONDARY SCHOOL SITE SURVEY - 2003

Deputy Headmaster Survey (PART 3)

<u>**Physical and Educational Resources**</u>

We appreciate your willingness to participate with Brigham Young University (U.S.A.) in conducting research addressing the role of resources in secondary schools in Uganda.
This School Site Survey is composed of three parts:
PART 1: Consent Form and Personnel Survey
Part 2: Headmaster Survey
Part 3: Deputy Headmaster Survey

We would appreciate your help and guidance in completing PART 3 of this survey under the direction of your Headmaster.

SCHOOL INFORMATION: **Please print your name and information about your school:**

School Name: _____
Interviewee Name: _____
Position: _____

SCHOOL LAND: **Please tell us about your school's land.**

2. What year was your land purchased or obtained? _____

3. What is the size of your school's property?   _____ Acres

4. Please describe how you use the land owned by the school:

Is land used for (circle one):		Size of Space in Acres	List crops and animals raised and sports played	Is the land shared with other schools for these purposes?
Agriculture	YES or NO			
Husbandry	YES or NO			
Sports	YES or NO			

5. How much of your land is currently undeveloped for school used? _____ Acres

Appendices

6. Please describe the physical location and condition of your school land (check one in each category).

a. **Useability:** ___ Mostly unuseable ___ Partially useable ___ Mostly useable

b. **Wetlands:** ___ No wetlands ___ Some wetlands ___ All wetlands

c. **Near Homes/Shops:** ___ Near few ___ Near some ___ Near many

d. **Paved Roads:** ___ Next to the school ___ Some nearby ___ Only few nearby

e. **Hilly or Flat:** ___ Flat ___ Somewhat Hilly ___ Very Hilly

f. **Land Cleared:** ___ Only slightly ___ Quite a bit ___ All

g. **Taxi access:** ___ Under 5 min. walk ___ 5-15 min walk
___ More than 15 minutes

7. Please describe the appearance of your school (check one in each category):

a. **Walkways:** ___ Mostly tarmac ___ Partially tarmac ___ None tarmac

b. **Front Gate**: ___ Locking ___ Gate, but not locking ___ No front gate

c. **Security guard:** ___ Visible from front ___ On premises, not always visible
___ No security guard

d. **Yard:** ___ Large grass area ___ Some grass area ___ No grass area

e. **Fencing**: ___ Entire compound ___ Partial compound ___ No fencing

f. **Physical Appearance**:

How often do parents comment **_positively_** on the physical appearance of your school?

1	2	3	4	5
Rarely	Occasionally	Sometimes	Often	Very Often

SCHOOL'S WATER: Please tell us about your school's water.

8. Describe your school's source of water:

a. YES NO Is your water source on your property (circle one)?
b. _____ If no, how far away is the water source (in kilometers)?
c. How do you transport water (circle all that apply):
Gerry cans   Buckets   Pumps   Other (specify) _____

d.   YES NO Do you have access to a well, a spring, or a bore hole?   e.
e.   YES NO Do you have tap water?
f.   How do you store your water (circle all that apply):
Cistern   Tanks   Gerry cans   Buckets   Other (specify) _____

g.   YES NO Do you have any system for capturing and storing rain water? Please describe:

h.   How do you purify your water (circle all that apply):
Boiling   Chemicals   No purification treatment

i.   How would you rate the quality of your water before purification (circle one)?

    1   2   3   4   5
  Poor   Moderate   Excellent

SCHOOL'S FUEL SOURCES: **Please tell us about your school's fuel sources.**

9.   Describe your schools fuel sources:

	Which of the following fuel sources are used by your school (mark all that apply):	Please rank these sources in order of importance for your school (1 = Most important):	What is the average cost of this fuel source for a month? (in UGS 000's)
Wood			
Petrol for Generator			
Petrol for Vehicles			
Natural Gas or Propane LP Gas			
Paraffin			

SCHOOL'S ELECTRICITY/LIGHT: **Please tell us about your school's resources for electricity and light.**

10.   YES NO   Is UEB your main supply of electricity (please circle)?

11.   What does your average electricity bill cost for a month (UGS 000's)?
_____

12.   How much do you agree or disagree that the cost of electricity causes you to limit its use?

    1   2   3   4   5
Strongly Disagree   Agree   Strongly Agree

13.   What alternative sources of electricity are available at the school (circle all that apply)?
a. Gas generator   b. Batteries   c: Solar   d: Other (please describe)

14. How often are alternative sources of electricity used (circle one)?
    a. About once a day   e. Every few months
    b. About once a week   f. About once a year
    c. Every few weeks   g. Never
    d. About once a month

15. What alternative sources of light are available at the school (circle all that apply)?
    a. Candles   b. Torch   c. Paraffin Lamps   d. Other (please describe): _____

HEALTH & SANITATION: Please tell us about your school's health and sanitation resources.

16. YES NO   Does the school have access to a nurse for students?

17. YES NO   Is the nurse a member of the school staff?

18. YES NO   Does the school have health clinic services available at the school?

19. YES NO   Does the school have flushing toilets? _____ How many?

20. YES NO   Does your school have separate pits/stances for girls & boys?

21. _____ How many stances (pits) does the school have?

22. _____ How many showers does the school have?

23. _____ How many wash areas (wash basin equivalents) does the school have?

School Resources and Performance in Developing Countries

TRANSPORTATION: Please describe your school's transportation.

23. YES NO Does the school own or have vehicles?
 (If no, skip diagram and go to question 24.)

	Vehicle Descriptions			
Describe each vehicle that the school owns (type, make, model)	1	2	3	4
Year of Vehicle				
Estimate of annual kilometers used for school business				
How many days a month is this vehicle used?				
Number of people that can be transported at one time				
Square meters of space that could be used for hauling supplies, etc. (e.g. truck bed)?				
Who services this vehicle and where?				
How many times a year do you service this vehicle?				
Date of last maintenance				
Estimate of maintenance cost per year				

24. _____ How many vehicles are owned personally by school staff yet used for school purposes?

25. YES NO Do you hire vehicles from other persons, schools organizations?

26. How often does the school hire or borrow a vehicle (circle one)?
 a. Daily   b. Once a week   c. Once a month   d. Every few months
 e. Never

27. For what reasons do you hire or borrow vehicles?
a. _____
b. _____

28. _____ How many bicycles are owned by the school for school use?

Appendices

COMMUNICATION: Please tell us about your school's communication equipment.

29. _____ How many different telephone numbers does the school support (including mobile phones)?
30. _____ In addition to school phones, how many faculty or staff generally have mobile phones with them?
31. YES NO   Does the school have a functioning FAX machine available?
32. YES NO   Is a reliable internet connection available at the school for admin/faculty/staff use?

33. YES NO   Does the school have an email address?
If the school has an email address and would share it with us, please list it here: _____

EDUCATIONAL RESOURCES: Please tell us about your educational resources.

34. Do you provide any of the following supplies for students?

g. YES NO Exercise Books
h. YES NO Writing Paper (other than exercise books)
i. YES NO Pens

35. Please describe the teaching supplies that your school provides to the students or uses for teaching activities.

Teaching Supplies	On average, how often do you replenish your supplies? (weeks, months, or terms)	How expensive is this resource? 1 = Not expensive 2 = Slightly 3 = Somewhat 4 = Very 5 = Extremely	How important is this resource? 1 = Not important 2 = Slightly 3 = Somewhat 4 = Very 5 = Extremely
Writing Paper (for teachers)			
Chalk			
Pencils & Pens			
Science Chemicals			
Hydrochloric Acid			
Sulfuric Acid			
Nitric Acid			
NaOH hydroxide			
Copper Sulfate			
Zinc Metal			
Sodium Metal			
Benedict Solution			

COMPUTER RESOURCES: Please tell us about your computer resources.

36. YES NO   Do you have computers available for student use? (If no, go to question 55.)

Please describe your school's involvement in computer training:

37. YES NO   Do you offer formal computer training as a subject?

38. _____ Approximately what percentage of your students receive any computer training?

39. _____ How many teachers know how to use a computer?

40. _____ How many different teachers participate in teaching computer courses for students?

41. _____ How many teachers have received external computer training or certification of some type?

Appendices

Please describe your school's computer resources that are available for student use:

42. _____ How many hours a week are computers available to A-Level students (in and out of class)?

43. _____ How many hours a week are computers available to O-Level students (in and out of class)?

44. _____ Do A-Level students use the computer to complete homework assignments?

45. _____ Do O-Level students use the computer to complete homework assignments?

46. _____ How many functioning printers does the school own?

47. _____ How many functioning computers do you have for student use?

48. YES NO   Are all the student computers in one location?

49. YES NO   Is the computer in a room that can be locked for security?

50. How many of these functioning computers were manufactured in the following time periods:
    _____ Pre 1995   _____ 1995-1999   _____ 2000-present

51. How many of these functioning computers for students have the following:
    _____ 3 ½" drives
    _____ Zip drives
    _____ CD drives
    _____ CD Burning Capability
    _____ Internet connection
    _____ Connecting to working printer

52. How many of these functioning computers for students have the following software functions:
    _____ Word Processing
    _____ Spreadsheet
    _____ Presentations or Slide Shows
    _____ Database
    _____ Games

53. Please describe your school's computer supplies:

Computer Supplies	Number as of today (count)	How long will current inventory last? (months)	How expensive is this resource? 1 = Not expensive 2 = Slightly 3 = Somewhat 4 = Very 5 = Extremely	How important is this resource? 1 = Not important 2 = Slightly 3 = Somewhat 4 = Very 5 = Extremely
Printer Paper (# reams of 500 sheets)				
New 3 ½" disks				
New Zip disks				
New CD-R's				

ATHLETIC RESOURCES:

54. Please describe the different athletic activities or sports supported by the school's facilities and equipment:

	Athletic/Sport Descriptions			
Name of Sport/Athletic Activity				
Does the school have a team that competes with other schools in this sport? Y/N				
If teams, has the school received awards or honors in this sport? Y/N				
Activity for (B) boys, (G) girls or (BG) both?				
Athletic equipment available for this sport or activity (e.g. counts):				
Balls				
Nets				
Hoops				
Goals				
Other:				

Appendices

VOCATIONAL RESOURCES:

55. Please describe any vocational resources at your school.

Vocational Activities (add additional activities if hey are not listed)	Which activities are provided by your School? (check)	Which activities are available for your students through another school or partnership? (Check) If yes, where?	List Resources that the School has to support these activities
Agriculture	Y N		
Woodworking	Y N		
Sewing/Tailoring	Y N		
Metalworking	Y N		
Husbandry	Y N		
Computer Studies	Y N		(Already listed in this survey.)
Electrician	Y N		

BUILDING BLOCKS: Please tell us about your school's buildings blocks.

56. Please describe your school's buildings:

a. ___Number of separate building blocks in your school
b. ___Number of buildings blocks currently under construction
c. ___Number of buildings blocks planned but not yet under construction
d. ___Number of buildings blocks with doors?
e. ___Number of buildings blocks with glass in windows?
f. ___Number of buildings blocks with cement floors (or other covering)?
g. ___Number of buildings blocks with electricity?

57. How many of your building blocks have the following exterior finishes:
a. ___ Brick   b. ___ Stucco   c. ___ Paint   d. Other (Specify): _____

58. Please describe how many of your building blocks have the following construction:
a. ___ Brick (self made)   b. ___ Brick (purchased)   c. Wood
d. Other (Specify): _____

155

59. How many classrooms for each grade level?

S1	S2	S3	S4	S5	S6

60. In the space below and if needed behind, please diagram your school's building blocks. Give each block a unique number and list the number of classrooms, administrative rooms, and laboratories each block contains. (The researcher will measure these by "pacing them off" during the course of the interview.)

   Name of Researcher Pacing: _____
   Length of Pace: _____ inches

Appendices

61. Please measure the following rooms and answer the questions in the table:

Size & Capacity of each of the following rooms:	Room	Size	Max Capacity
-Classrooms (S1-S6) **-1 Dormitory (D1)** **-Science Laboratory (SL1)** **-Library (L1)** **-1 Administrative Room (A1)** Size =(**meters x meters** e.g. 6.21 x 4.25) Max Capacity (only for classrooms & dorms) = # of persons seated or boarded)	S1		
	S2		
	S3		
	S4		
	S5		
	S6		
	D1		
	SL1		
	L1		
	A1		
Total Internal Size (sq. ft) Calculate from previous question (later)			
Type of Room		How many rooms does the school utilize for the following purposes?	
Administrative			
Dormitory/ Student Boarding			
Library			
Food Prep/Sto rage			
Meeting Hall			
Computer Lab/Room			
Science Laboratory			
Faculty/Staff Area			
Faculty/Staff Boarding			
Husbandry			
Storage/ Tools			
Dining Area			
Garage			
Entertainment			
Health & Medical			
Security			
Hall for National Exams			

School Resources and Performance in Developing Countries

LIBRARY RESOURCES: Please describe the books and library resources in your school.

62. YES   NO   Do students read in the library (please circle)?

63. In what places do the students usually read?

64. (To be done by the research assistants) ---- Estimate "other" books available to the school that teachers, administrators or school students keep in their possession. This is not book loans to other schools.

Library Resources	School-owned Books in Library (estimate number of books in library)	School-owned Books with Teachers (estimate number held by teachers & NOT in library)	School-owned Books with Administrators (estimate number held by administrators & NOT in library)	School-owned Books with Students (estimate number held by school's students & NOT in library)
Number of Books (count)				
Overall Condition of Books 1 = Poor 2 = Fair 3 = Good 4 = Very Good 5 = Excellent				

65. What are the copyright dates on 10 books?

Random Check for Age of Books- Instructions for Research Assistants:
Pick the 1st book on a shelf in the school's library. Write down the copyright year from the front pages into one of the boxes below. Go about 3 feet of books to the right and select a 2nd book. Continue through the shelves in a methodical, non-duplicating manner, until you have 10 books. If you run out of shelf space, begin again 1 foot to the right of your previous beginning point and go every 3 feet until you have 10 books.

Appendices

APPENDIX B (CONTINUED)
SECONDARY SCHOOL SITE SURVEY – 2003
Additional Information Resource Survey (PART 4)
Student Intake, UNEB Exam, & Class/School Timetable Information

SCHOOL INFORMATION: Please complete the following demographic information:

School Name: _____
Your Name: _____
Post: _____

Please tick one of the following school types:
Government_____   Private_____   Community_____

STUDENT INTAKE INFORMATION: Please describe the school's student intake for 1999-2002:

1. Please name up to five primary schools that send the largest number of primary students to your school:
   a. _____
   b. _____
   c. _____
   d. _____
   e. _____

2. Please provide one of the following: either COPIES of the PLE and O-level exam admission scores for the students accepted to your school through the years 1999-2002 or INDICATE the mean PLE and O-level exam admission scores for the years 1999-2002:
   a. 1999: _____ _____   b. 2000: _____ _____
   c. 2001: _____ _____   d. 2002: _____ _____
             PLE   O-level   PLE   O-level

UNEB EXAM INFORMATION: Please provide information in reference to UNEB O/A-level exams:

3. Do other secondary schools send students to your school to sit for the UNEB O/A-level exams? Please circle: Yes or No

4. If yes, please name up to three secondary schools that send students to your school to sit for the UNEB O/A-level exams:
   a. _____
   b. _____
   c. _____

School Resources and Performance in Developing Countries

5. Does your school send students to sit for the UNEB O/A-level exams at other secondary schools? Please circle: Yes or No

6. If yes, please name up to three secondary schools where your school sends students to sit for the UNEB O/A-level exams:
    a. _____
    b. _____
    c. _____

CLASS/SCHOOL TIMETABLE INFORMATION: Please describe the class timetable for the school.

7. Please indicate the amount of time allocated to the following areas:
    a. Minutes per Lesson _____
    b. Time per Chemistry Practical: _____ (hours per week)
    c. Time per Biology Practical: _____ (hours per week)
    d. Time per Physics Practical: _____ (hour per week)

8. Please indicate how often science practicals are conducted per week:
    a. Chemistry: _____ b. Biology: _____ c. Physics: _____

9. Please indicate how many hours per week your students spend in the library: _____

10. Please indicate how often parent teacher association meetings take place: Please circle one of the following:
    a. weekly   b. monthly   c. once each term   d. once each year   e. never
    f. other: _____